Dear Parents:

Welcome to the Boy Scouts of America. Tiger Cubs is the beginning of what we hope will become a lasting relationship between your son and the Scouting program. **Scouting is fun with a purpose.** Through his participation in the Scouting program, and with your guidance, your son will be well on his way toward developing strong character, good citizenship, and healthy personal fitness habits.

The Tiger Cub program is designed to meet the needs of the youngest members of the BSA. Your son will be greatly helped by your enthusiastic participation in the many parent-son activities that are the core of the Tiger Cub program.

All parents want their children to enjoy a safe childhood. Part of growing up is learning how to avoid dangers. When children are the age of Tiger Cubs, parents are the most effective teachers of safety strategies.

Although discussing child safety issues with your children may sometimes be difficult for you, it is important. One of the most important steps parents can take to protect their children is to discuss defense strategies with them and to establish an atmosphere of open communication. Research shows that children whose parents talk to them about child protection are more effective at fending off assaults. Your role is very important.

The following points are offered to help you and your child talk about child protection issues:

- **If you are uncomfortable discussing child protection issues with your child, let him know.** When parents who are uncomfortable discussing safety with their children try to hide their uneasiness, the children may misinterpret the anxiety and be less likely to come to their parents when they need help. You can use a simple statement like, "I wish we did not have to talk about this. I am uncomfortable because I don't like to think that this could happen to you. I want you to know that it's important, and you can come to me whenever you have a question or if anybody ever tries to harm you."

- **Select words that your child understands.** Establishing an understanding between you and your child on safety issues makes it more likely that your child will come to you if something harmful happens.

- **Provide the opportunity for your child to practice youth protection skills.** Learning is made more effective when children have the chance to practice with you the skills they are taught.

Personal Safety Rules for Children

Cub Scout–age children benefit from having concrete safety rules. It is important, however, to stress that traditional cautions about "strangers" are not sufficient to protect our children. It may be hard for a child to differentiate between a stranger and someone who is known but not considered a trusted adult. In addition, individuals who harm children are usually known to the child. Cub Scout–age children need to rely upon adult guidance to improve their safety.

Discuss the following safety rules with your child and then help your child apply them in the What if … exercises in the next section.

1. ***Check first with a parent or other trusted adult before you change plans, go anywhere, or accept anything from anyone.*** Children need to understand that their safety is greater when parents or the adult responsible for caring for them knows where they are and what they are doing.

2. ***Go with a friend in order to be safer and to have more fun.*** For Cub Scouts, the friend should be a parent, other trusted adult, or older child.

3. ***It is your body and you have the right to say no to anyone who tries to touch you in places covered by your swimming suit or to do things that you think are wrong.*** Children need to be empowered to set personal limits and to resist anyone who fails to respect those limits.

4. ***Tell a trusted adult anytime you are hurt, scared, or made to feel uncomfortable.*** Cub Scouts need help in recognizing whom they should trust. Parents are in the best position to help children identify the adults in their lives deserving this trust. You can also reassure your child that he or she will not be in trouble when they come to you for help. It's very important that children understand they are not at fault when an adult or older child harms them.

Personal Safety Rules for Online Users

Most Cub Scout–age children are learning to use the Internet for schoolwork and for the many fun things available for children on the Internet. Children need to learn that in addition to many acceptable uses, using the Internet can place them in danger if they don't follow the rules. The NetSmartz Studio, a subsidiary of the National Center for Missing & Exploited Children, suggests that Cub Scout–age children make the following pledge:

1. I will talk with my parents or guardian so we can set up rules for going online. The rules will include the time of day I may be online, the length of time I may be online, whom I may communicate with while online, and appropriate areas for me to visit while online. I will not break these rules or access other areas without their permission.

2. I will tell a trusted adult if I come across anything that makes me feel scared, uncomfortable, or confused. I will not download anything from anyone without permission from my parents or guardian.

3. I will never share personal information such as my address, my telephone number, my parents' or guardian's work address/telephone number, or the name and location of my school without my parents' or guardian's permission.

4. I will never respond to any messages that are mean or in any way make me feel uncomfortable. If I do get a message like that, I will tell a trusted adult right away so he or she can contact the online service. And I will not send those kinds of messages.

5. I will never meet in person with anyone I have first "met" online without checking with my parents or guardian. If my parents or guardian agrees to the meeting, it will be in a public place and my parents or guardian must come along.

A Bobcat Requirement

Helping your son learn to apply these personal safety rules can be approached in the same non-frightening way you teach him not to play with fire or to look both ways when he crosses the

> Fulfilling these requirements completes 🐾 on the Bobcat trail (see page 162).

street. Discussing the following situations with your son offers an opportunity for you to help your child learn how to apply the rules and to complete a requirement for his Bobcat award—the first step in his Cub Scout advancement.

"What if . . ." Situations and Applicable Safety Rules

What if you are playing in your yard and your neighbor asks you to help carry groceries into his house? What should you do?

- *Check first with a parent or other trusted adult before you change plans, go anywhere, or accept anything from anyone.*

What if you are camping with a relative and he suggests that you allow him to take your picture when you are not wearing clothes? What do you do?

- Tell your relative that you do not want to have your picture taken. *(It is your body and you have the right to say no to anyone who tries to touch you in places covered by your swimming suit or to do things that you think are wrong.)*

- Tell your parents when you return home what happened. *(Tell a trusted adult anytime you are hurt, scared, or made to feel uncomfortable.)*

What if you are playing at a friend's house and his older brother and some of his friends invite you to join a club? To join the club you are expected to take off all your clothes and wrestle with them. Your friend wants to join. What do you do?

- Tell your friend it's time for you to go home; leave immediately. *(It's your body and you have the right to say no to anyone who wants to touch you in places covered by your swimming suit or to do things that you think are wrong.)*

- When you get home, explain to your parents what happened. *(Tell a trusted adult anytime you are hurt, scared, or made to feel uncomfortable.)*

What if a neighbor comes to you and says your mother is sick and you must go with him? This neighbor is not a person you have been told it's OK to go with. What would you do?

- Check first with a parent or other trusted adult before you change plans, go anywhere, or accept anything from anyone.

   — If at school, go to the principal or your teacher for help and verification.

   — If at home or somewhere else, call the emergency number—parents' employers, close relative—for help and verification.

   — Don't go anywhere without checking with someone in authority whom you have been told to contact in this kind of situation.

What if you are in a public restroom and someone tries to touch your private parts? What do you do?

- Yell "STOP THAT" as loudly as you can and run out of the room as quickly as possible. *(It's your body and you have the right to say no to anyone who tries to touch you in places covered by your swimming suit or to do things that you think are wrong.)*

- Tell your parent, a police officer, a security guard, or other adult (such as your teacher) what happened. *(Tell a trusted adult anytime you are hurt, scared, or made to feel uncomfortable.)*

What if you are walking to school in the rain and a car stops and the driver asks if you want a ride? What do you do?

- Stay away from the car; you do not need to go close to the car to answer.

- Unless you have your parent's permission to ride with the person, say "No, thank you." If the driver persists, say "No!" *(Check first with a parent or other trusted adult before you change plans, go anywhere, or accept anything from anyone.)*

- Tell your teacher when you get to school, and tell your parent when you get home. *(Tell a trusted adult anytime you are hurt, scared, or made to feel uncomfortable.)*

What if you are playing on the playground and an adult comes up to you and asks you to help find his or her lost puppy? What do you do?

- Adults should ask other adults for help. Tell the person you have to ask for permission. *(Check first with a parent or other trusted adult before you change plans, go anywhere, or accept anything from anyone.)*

- Tell your parent what happened. *(Tell a trusted adult anytime you are hurt, scared, or made to feel uncomfortable.)*

What if your babysitter asks you to sit on her lap while she reads a story and shows you pictures of naked people?

- Tell her no. *(You have the right to say no to anyone who wants you to do things that you think are wrong.)*

- Tell your parent what happened. *(Tell a trusted adult anytime you are hurt, scared, or made to feel uncomfortable.)*

What if you're using the Internet and a pop up asks you to fill out a form with your name, address, birth date, and telephone number to win a prize?

- Do not give out personal information on the Internet. You never can tell how it will be used or even who will get it. *(Check first with a parent or other trusted adult before you change plans, go anywhere, or accept anything from anyone.)*

Fulfilling these requirements completes 🐾 on the Bobcat trail (see page 162).

Welcome to the Tiger Cub Handbook

Contents

TIGER CUB

Illustrations of T.C. by Robert Depew

34713
ISBN 0-8395-4713-7
© 2001 Boy Scouts of America
2008 Printing

Introductory Guide for Tiger Cub Adult Partners

Helping Your Son Along the Trail...

Your son is growing up fast. Just look at how quickly he outgrows his clothes! Ten years from now, he'll be 16 or 17 years old. Wow!

As he is growing, you can give him something that can help him develop self-assurance as he builds respect for other people. And he and you will both have fun doing it.

This adventure with him begins with **Tiger Cubs**—a program of exciting indoor and outdoor activities just right for a boy who is in first grade and/or is 7 years old. You are there with him as his support and guide, but you don't do things *for* him. He will learn by doing things *himself.* And as he learns and grows, your relationship with him will grow, too.

At the end of the school year, he will graduate into a Wolf Cub Scout den. Later, he will be in a Bear den, and then he'll become a Webelos Scout. After 12 to 18 months as a Webelos Scout, he will move on to the adventure of Boy Scouting; where he can earn the Eagle Scout rank, the highest rank in Boy Scouting.

Using This Handbook

Your Tiger Cub and you, his adult partner, are a *team*. This handbook is for both of you. Much of what is in it, such as this introductory guide, is for you, the adult. But you will also find basic information in it (for instance, "Welcome to Tiger Cubs," page 25) for you to read with your Tiger Cub. Furthermore, you will read the advancement activities with him as he prepares to work on each one. And you will find "Did You Know?" facts—information about Tiger Cubs and the Boy Scouts of America that is intended for you, but that your son may also find interesting.

This introductory guide gives you an overview of Tiger Cubs, including information about dens, leadership, uniforms, and advancement, as well as ideas for planning a den program. After that are the advancement activities—achievements and electives. Finally, there are sections on Cub Scouting's Leave No Trace Awareness Award, the Cub Scout Outdoor Activity Award, the Cub Scout Academics and Sports program, Cub Scouting's BSA Family Program, and the transition into a Wolf Cub Scout den.

Your Son, Scouting, and You

As a parent or caring adult, you want your son to grow up to be self-reliant and dependable, worthy and caring. Scouting has these same goals in mind for him.

> The purpose of the Boy Scouts of America is to provide an educational program for boys and young adults to build desirable qualities of character, to train in the responsibilities of participating citizenship, and to develop personal fitness. Personal fitness includes physical, mental, and emotional fitness.

Since 1910 the BSA has been weaving lifetime values into fun and educational activities. These activities are designed to help families teach their sons how to make good decisions throughout their lives and give them confidence as they become the adult leaders of tomorrow. Tiger Cubs gives you opportunities to share your ideals, values, and dreams with your son.

As a Tiger Cub, your son will be part of a group of boys his own age called a *den*. With his den, he can build confidence and self-esteem and earn recognition. He will also gain a sense of personal achievement from the new skills he learns. As a team, you and your son will *search* out new activities, *discover* new things, and *share* them with others. This is following the Tiger Cub concept of "Search, discover and share," around which Tiger Cub den meetings are built.

These days, boys are often taught that winning is everything. But Tiger Cubs teaches them to *do their best* and to *be helpful to others.* This is expressed in the Cub Scout Promise, the Cub Scout motto, and the Law of the Pack, which he will learn as he earns his Bobcat badge before starting along the Tiger Cub Badge Trail. (See page 163.)

Tiger Cubs: How Does It Work?

Your Tiger Cub will be a member of a *den.* Most dens have five to nine boy–adult partner *teams,* meet twice a month in a den meeting, and have one outing a month, called a *Go See It.* The den also takes part in the monthly pack meetings (see page 6). During den meetings, Go See It outings, and pack meetings, boys learn new things and have fun.

Each den meeting and den activity is led by a *den leader* and an *adult partner* of one of the Tiger Cubs. An adult partner can be a parent, relative, or friend who is at least 18 years old. The adult partner attends all den meetings, pack meetings, outings, and activities with the Tiger Cub, and may register as an adult leader in the pack. Each adult partner takes a turn working with the den leader to plan and lead a den meeting and/or activity. (You'll read more about this *shared leadership* on page 6.)

Your Tiger Cub is also a member of a Cub Scout *pack.* Most packs are made up of several dens that gather monthly at a *pack meeting.* Pack meetings usually follow a suggested theme and are a time for boys to be recognized for their accomplishments during the month, to perform skits and songs they have learned in den meetings, and to have fun with the entire family.

Packs are led by a *Cubmaster* and *pack committee.* Like the den leaders, the Cubmaster and assistants are volunteer leaders and are usually family members of boys in the pack. The pack committee makes plans for pack meetings and activities and takes care of the "business" items that are necessary for a pack to operate smoothly.

Most pack committees consist of family members and members of the pack's *chartered organization.* The chartered organization is the community organization that is granted a charter by the BSA local council to use the Scouting program. This chartered organization might be a school, service club, religious group, or other group interested in youth. The chartered organization approves the leadership of the pack, provides a meeting place, and operates the pack within the guidelines and policies of that organization and the BSA.

When Do Tiger Cubs Meet?

To experience the fun, excitement, and other benefits of Cub Scouting, you and your Tiger Cub will do the following things each month:

- **Go to two one-hour den meetings at the host adult partner's home or other location.** Leaders will try to hold the meetings at a time that is convenient for all adult partners and is appropriate for boys of Tiger Cub age. Some dens meet at a school, a place of worship, or the location of their chartered organization. But meetings can be held almost anywhere—in a basement, recreation center, backyard, or park—as long as the meeting location is safe for boys and their families.

- **Take a field trip, or Go See It, with the entire den.** The Go See It is a planned field trip to a place that is interesting to boys. It may be associated with the monthly theme (see "Using the Monthly Theme in the Den Meeting," page 8) or one of the advancement requirements.

- **Attend the Cub Scout pack meeting.**

What Is Shared Leadership?

The success of a Tiger Cub den depends on active, enthusiastic families and a knowledgeable, well-trained den leader. The den leader plans and carries out a year-round program of activities for the Tiger Cub den and gives continuity to the program. Each month, however, the den leader also works with a different boy–adult partner team to plan the two monthly den meetings, the Go See It, and the den's part in the pack meeting. (Some teams may serve more than one month, depending on how big the den is.) This is called **shared leadership.**

Shared leadership is a key part of Tiger Cubs because the direct involvement of you and other adults is important for boys at this age. Shared leadership also gives each boy and adult partner a chance to lead, often resulting in an interesting variety of activities as each boy–adult partner team shares its knowledge and resources.

Uniforms

The uniform is an important part of the Scouting program. It identifies the boys and adults with Tiger Cubs and gives them a sense of belonging to the den, the pack, and the Boy Scouts of America. Most boys enjoy wearing their Tiger Cub uniform. They should wear it to all den meetings, pack meetings, and special pack activities.

The uniform for the Tiger Cub is the official blue pants or shorts and a blue shirt with appropriate Tiger Cub insignia. There is a blue belt with a Tiger Cub buckle, and an orange and blue neckerchief with a slide. You also wear an official navy blue cap with orange front panel and Tiger Cub emblem. Adult partners don't have to wear a uniform, but it is highly recommended that they wear a Tiger Cub orange T-shirt. The Tiger Cub den leader wears the official Cub Scout leader uniform, the Tiger Cub cap, and the Tiger Cub leader neckerchief.

Planning the Tiger Cub Den Meeting

With shared leadership, each month a different boy–adult partner works with the Tiger Cub den leader to plan the two monthly den meetings and the Go See It. Together, they also organize the participation of the den at the monthly pack meeting. It is important that each boy–adult partner team has a turn at planning and conducting the den activities.

The den meetings will be based on the theme of the month (see "Using the Monthly Theme in the Den Meeting" below) or on one of the den activity parts of an achievement. (You'll read

The Tiger Cub Den Meeting Program form, found in the *Cub Scout Leader Book*, helps leaders and boy–adult partner teams plan weekly Tiger Cub meetings.

more about the three parts of achievements below.)

The Tiger Cub den leader and the host adult partner can also use the resources of other families in the den for den activities. Let the boys give their ideas, too. See "Tiger Cub Den Resources" on page 13 for creative program ideas.

Remember: A well-planned den meeting will hold the boys' interest, and they will be excited to return.

Using the Monthly Theme in the Den Meeting

Each year, ***Cub Scout Program Helps*** (No. 34304) suggests 12 monthly themes suitable for Tiger Cubs and Cub Scouts. This annual publication includes songs, skits, games, crafts, and ideas for Go See It activities that complement the theme. ***Boys' Life*** magazine also features ideas and articles each month on the recommended theme, and

Possible Monthly Themes

All Aboard!: All about trains

Blast Off!: Rocket ships, space program

Circus Fun: Three-ring circus with animals and acts

Exciting Explorers: Famous adventurers and their accomplishments

Hometown Heroes: Recognize people who make a difference in your community.

Land Before Time: Dinosaurs

Magic: Secrets of the magicians' art, amazing feats

Rodeo: A look at the Wild West

Treasure Chest: Pirates

Visiting Other Lands: Cultures from around the world

the monthly Cub Scout roundtables provide program ideas and instruction for these same themes.

Packs aren't required to use the recommended theme each month, but they are chosen and planned to appeal to boys and to offer opportunities for them, and you, to achieve the purposes of Cub Scouting (see page 21 for more about the purposes of Cub Scouting). By following the themes, den leaders and the Cubmaster have a lot of support material available to them.

Tiger Cub den leaders and host adult partners introduce the theme at the first den meeting of the month. The activities for the second den meeting and the pack meeting also use the monthly theme. Therefore, the theme provides continuity among the two den meetings, the Go See It, and the pack meeting. The theme is different each month, which helps provide variety and hold the boys' interest.

Cub Scout Program Helps includes den meeting charts with ideas for den meetings based on the monthly theme.

Parts of a Tiger Cub Den Meeting

The focus of every den meeting plan should be based on the Tiger Cub idea of: *search, discover,* and *share.* The Tiger Cub den meeting plan in *Cub Scout Program Helps* divides the meeting into eight parts. Each part has a purpose, so the den meeting will be better for the boys if you follow this pattern. It will make planning and running the den meetings easier.

> ## Parts of a Tiger Cub Den Meeting
> 1. Before the Meeting
> 2. Gathering
> 3. Opening
> 4. Share
> 5. Discover
> 6. Search
> 7. Closing
> 8. After the Meeting

1. **Before the meeting.** The purpose of this part of the meeting is to give the den leader and the host adult partner time to make preparations, gather supplies, set out the U.S. flag, and take care of any last-minute details before the boys and their adult partners arrive.

2. The **Gathering** is an activity or game that keeps the boys interested and busy while everybody else arrives. Planning activities for when Tiger Cubs arrive will help avoid some of the behavior problems that can happen when boys don't have enough to do. The gathering time also gives the den leader time to take attendance, collect dues, and keep track of the achievements each boy has completed while the host adult partner is with the boys.

3. The **Opening** is the official start of the den meeting. Whereas the gathering time is an informal time, the opening is an organized activity that signals the beginning of the meeting. Here are some ideas:

- Most den meetings begin with a flag ceremony. At this time, the boys can practice saying the Cub Scout Promise. (See page 29.)

- A brief prayer may be included, but always be sensitive to the diverse religious beliefs that may be represented in the den.

- The opening may also include boisterous action or a song.

- A roll call isn't necessary, but boys like to hear their names being said. If the meeting relates to a monthly theme, such as jungle animals, each boy could respond with the name of a jungle animal.

4. The **Share** part of the den meeting gives each boy an opportunity to share something that he has done since the last meeting. This activity gives boys time to share family experiences.

5. For the **Discover** time, the den leader may introduce the monthly theme and talk about what the den will be doing for the pack meeting. Then, the boys will play games, work on craft projects and puzzles, take part in outdoor activities, or work on advancement requirements. Once your Tiger Cub has done his best, you can approve the completion of the requirement and the den leader will record his progress in the den records. See more about advancement on page 14.)

Den activities that boys and their adult partners can do together are the best. They are a team, so they should participate and have fun as a team.

Boys love to play games, so each meeting should include at least one game. It can be indoors or outdoors, quiet or active. The host Tiger Cub could lead the game. Once again, adult partners should be included.

Sometimes, boys will do a craft project during a den meeting. For instance, around the holidays, boys could do holiday-related crafts or make something that is needed for the pack meeting. Some projects can be completed during one or two den meetings, but others might require that you and your Tiger Cub work together at home The den leader and host adult partner can explain the project and help the boys do it. (You and other adult partners can be very helpful during craft time.)

6. During the **Search** time of the meeting, the leaders will talk about plans for the Go See It. Boys love to get out and see new things. This activity could fulfill one of the achievement requirements or one of the elective requirements, and/or it could relate to the monthly theme.

7. The **Closing** period draws the meeting to an end and is usually more serious and quiet. Den leaders might present a thought for the day, have the boys say the Cub Scout Promise or the Law of the Pack together (see pages 29 and 31), and/or give everyone last-minute reminders about upcoming events. Leaders can also use this time to reinforce the 12 core values of Cub Scouting (you'll read about the 12 core values on page 23).

8. **After the Meeting,** the den leader and host adult partner review the events of the meeting and finalize plans for the next meeting and the upcoming pack meeting. If this is the second den meeting of the month, the den leader may meet with the host adult partner for the next month to plan and/or preview that month's den activities.

The Tiger Cub Den Meeting Program form (illustrated on page 8) helps the den leader and host adult partner plan a den meeting. A few days before the den meeting, they fill in the details for each portion of the den meeting, including the plan and the supplies and equipment needed.

For the Den Leader and Host Adult Partner: Tiger Cub Den Resources and Den Tools

Several resources are available to help the Tiger Cub den leader and host adult partner plan and run the den meetings and the Go See It. Some of them may be available through your pack library.

- Most important, each Tiger Cub–adult partner team should have a copy of this book, the *Tiger Cub Handbook* (No. 34713). It describes how Tiger Cubs work, including advancement information and requirements.

- Another important book is called the *Cub Scout Leader Book* (No. 33221). Your den and pack leaders can refer to it for accurate information about Cub Scouting. This book also contains a chapter on Tiger Cubs, as well as the needed Tiger Cub report forms.

- *Cub Scout Program Helps* (No. 34304) has den meeting outlines based on the monthly themes. The activities planned for Tiger Cubs and their adult partners are age-appropriate for first-grade boys.

- The *Cub Scout Leader How-To Book* (No. 33832) is filled with ideas for games, crafts, skits, songs, stories, and much more.

- Check your pack library or council service center for materials on songs, ceremonies, family programs, the Cub Scout Academics and Sports program, and outdoor opportunities that you could use with your den.
- The den should have a Tiger Cub den flag and a U.S. flag for opening and closing ceremonies. These may be furnished by the pack, along with flag stands.
- Dens will need items for projects and games. Since the den meeting place may be different each month, it can be a good idea to have a "travel box" that goes to each den site. It could include things such as crayons, paint, paintbrushes, glue, scissors, paper, rulers, pencils, wood pieces, cord or string, spools, plastic bottle caps, jar lids, aluminum foil, leather scraps, beads, craft feathers, and fabric. Den families could donate or loan these.

Advancement

In Scouting, **advancement** is the process by which a member meets certain requirements and earns recognition. Boys in Cub Scouting work on advancement with their families. The Tiger Cub advancement program is a blend of activities boys do in their home and activities they do in a den setting with their adult partner. This is unique to Tiger Cubs.

No matter what age or grade a boy joins Cub Scouting, he must earn his Bobcat badge before he can be awarded a Tiger Cub badge, Wolf badge, Bear badge, or Webelos badge. Help your Tiger Cub through the steps of the Bobcat trail. Along each step, sign "Akela's OK." The den leader will also sign and indicate your boy's completion on the Den Advancement Report, which he or she will also give to the pack committee at the monthly pack leaders' meeting. Along the Bobcat trail, your son will earn the Tiger Cub Immediate Recognition emblem for completing three specified requirements. When all of the other Bobcat requirements have been completed, your boy is then eligible to receive his Bobcat badge in a pack ceremony.*

Akela (ah-KAY-la) means "good leader." As your boy's adult partner, you are Akela.

A Tiger Cub may earn the **Tiger Cub rank.** This rank is for those boys who are in first grade or are 7 years old. All the Cub Scout ranks (Tiger Cub, Wolf, Bear, Webelos, and Arrow of Light) are tailored for a grade and the corresponding age level.

To advance, Tiger Cubs work on *achievements* and *electives,* which are described in this handbook. As a boy completes these, to the best of his ability, you, his adult partner, sign in this handbook where it says "Akela's OK." Akela means "good leader" and is an important part of Cub Scouting. Akela can be a den leader, a teacher, or other important adult. As your boy's adult partner, you are Akela.

As boys advance, they are awarded *recognition items* to mark their progress. These items will be presented to them during a simple ceremony at a pack or den meeting. It is important for boys to be recognized for the good work they do. The Tiger Cub recognition items are the *Tiger Cub Immediate Recognition Emblem,* the *Tiger Cub badge,* and *Tiger Track beads.* (Although participation

---

* The Boy Scouts of America **prohibits** any Bobcat ceremony in which boys are physically turned upside down.

with an adult partner is required for all Tiger Cub awards, adult partners do not earn these awards. Recognition items are for boys only.)

Let's look at each of these and how boys earn them.

Tiger Cub Immediate Recognition Emblem

Along the Bobcat trail, a boy earns the Tiger Cub Immediate Recognition emblem by completing three specified Bobcat requirements.

- Learn the Cub Scout motto: *Do Your Best.*
- Learn the Cub Scout sign. (See page 32.)
- Learn the Cub Scout salute. (See page 34.)

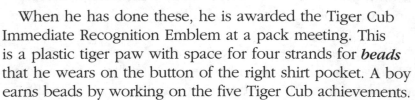

Cub Scout Motto
Do Your Best.

When he has done these, he is awarded the Tiger Cub Immediate Recognition Emblem at a pack meeting. This is a plastic tiger paw with space for four strands for *beads* that he wears on the button of the right shirt pocket. A boy earns beads by working on the five Tiger Cub achievements.

Achievements and Beads

There are five achievements in Tiger Cubs:

- Making My Family Special
- Where I Live
- Keeping Myself Healthy and Safe
- How I Tell It
- Let's Go Outdoors

Each achievement has three parts: a family activity, a den activity, and a Go See It outing. A boy receives totem beads as he completes each part:

- He earns a *white bead* for each required family activity part he completes.

- He earns an *orange bead* for each required den activity part he completes.

- He earns a *black bead* for each required Go See It part he completes.

These beads go on the first three strands of the Tiger Cub Immediate Recognition Emblem. (The fourth strand is for Tiger Track beads—see page 18.)

A boy can earn only one bead for each of the 15 achievement parts, regardless of how many times he may repeat a part.

As each bead is awarded and added to the boy's Immediate Recognition Emblem, he should be recognized with a simple ceremony at a den meeting. When a boy has earned all 15 beads, he is eligible to receive his Tiger Cub badge, signifying that he has earned the Tiger Cub rank.

Tiger Cub Badge

The Tiger Cub badge is awarded when boys have completed all 15 parts of the five achievements, that is, five family activities, five den activities, and five Go See It outings. During an impressive ceremony, the Tiger Cub badge is presented to the adult partner at a pack meeting, who in turn presents the badge to the boy. The badge is worn in the appropriate place on the left uniform pocket.

While your boy is working on advancement, you should be a part of the process. Family involvement is an integral part of the advancement process, which provides opportunities for you to participate in activities that are age-appropriate for your child. Besides signing his handbook as Akela once he has done his best, let your den leader know of any completed parts of achievements at your next den meeting. The den leader will keep a record of your boy's individual progress on the Tiger Cub Den Advancement Chart. In addition, your boy, with your help, will keep track of his own advancement on the Tiger Cub Badge Trail chart found on pages 163 of this handbook. This encourages him and helps him see his progress toward the Tiger Cub rank.

The advancement requirements are written in such a way as to give you room to customize activities for your boy and your den. There are no performance requirements for Tiger Cubs. Boys should never be "tested" or placed in a position where they will not be successful. *Simply participating in the activities and doing his best constitutes completion.*

The den activities and Go See It outings are intended to be completed with the den. If a Tiger Cub is unable to participate in an activity because of illness or a conflict, however, you may work with him to complete, to the best of his ability, these requirements. For your boy to receive the full benefit of the program, it is important for you, his adult partner, to make every effort to attend meetings regularly.

Electives and Tiger Track Beads

After your boy has earned the Tiger Cub badge, he can earn Tiger Track beads by completing elective activities in this handbook. The Tiger Cub program strives to provide an opportunity for your boy to learn and grow while having fun along with you. The wide variety of electives allows your Tiger Cub to choose additional activities and receive recognition for his participation. The electives help broaden a boy's horizons and fulfill the concept of Search, discover, and share. Electives provide advancement opportunities and recognition for your boy until he is eligible to begin working on the Wolf rank.

A boy shouldn't feel, however, that he must do all of the electives. Some may not appeal to him, and some he may want to do more than once. If a boy completes an elective activity twice, it may be counted as two electives. But at the same time, try to avoid much repetition, as variety will keep Tiger Cubs more interesting for your boy.

As with the achievements, you, the adult partner, approve your boy's completion of electives to the best of his ability by signing the handbook in the space provided for "Akela's OK." Then let your den leader know about completed electives. The den leader will fill in the Tiger Cub Den Advancement Report, found in the *Cub Scout Leader Book*, to show Tiger Track beads earned and give the report to the pack committee at the monthly pack leaders' meeting. In addition, your boy, with your help, will keep track of his own elective advancement on the Tiger Track Trail found on page 164 of this handbook.

Here's how earning Tiger Track beads works: A boy earns one Tiger Track bead for every 10 electives he completes. The Tiger Track bead is presented to you, the adult partner, at a pack meeting, and you in turn present it to your boy.

A boy may work concurrently on both achievement and elective projects; however, he can't receive Tiger Track beads until he has earned the Tiger Cub badge.

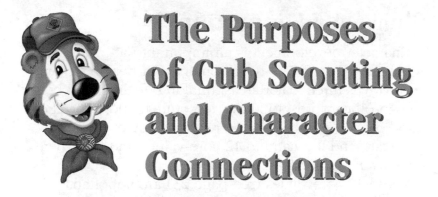

The Purposes of Cub Scouting and Character Connections

After your Tiger Cub completes an activity to the best of his ability, take the opportunity to talk with him and reflect on the experience. The purposes of Cub Scouting and Character Connections can help you do this. You will find Character Connection discussion questions in five of the achievement parts below.

The Purposes of Cub Scouting

Tiger Cubs is the first step of Cub Scouting, which the Boy Scouts of America offers for boys in first through fifth grade (or who are 7, 8, 9, or 10 years old). Parents, leaders, and organizations work together to achieve the 10 purposes of Cub Scouting:

1. Character Development
2. Spiritual Growth
3. Good Citizenship
4. Sportsmanship and Fitness
5. Family Understanding
6. Respectful Relationships
7. Personal Achievement
8. Friendly Service
9. Fun and Adventure
10. Preparation for Boy Scouts

Character Connections®

Character development is an important part of the Scouting program. The development of a person's character involves three major areas: thinking, feeling, and behavior—in other words, to know, to commit, and to practice. Cub Scouting emphasizes the relationships of the head, the heart, and the hand to 12 core values and calls them *Character Connections.*

These 12 core values (see page 23) are important throughout Tiger Cubs. Five of them, however—*responsibility, citizenship, health and fitness, respect,* and *faith*—are emphasized in the five achievements that your son will do during his Tiger Cub year (see pages 36-77). As you guide your Tiger Cub through these achievements, you will help him reflect on the three dimensions of character—know, commit, and practice. The Character Connections will ask the Tiger Cub to consider the following:

Know. What do I think or know? (What do I know about the core value, about the experience, about the context?)

Commit. How do I feel? (How do I feel about this value? What makes this difficult to do? How did this experience make me feel?)

Practice. What can I do? (How can I practice this value at school, at home, or with my friends?)

When your Tiger Cub is working on his achievements, take a few moments with him and help him think about and answer the Character Connection questions that follow the achievement activities. You don't have to spend a lot of time doing this, and it doesn't have to be complicated. It's an opportunity for you to add meaning to your boy's activities by encouraging him to think about them. You can also discuss your values with him.

The Character Connection questions are part of the achievement and must be completed before your Tiger Cub receives an immediate recognition bead for that activity.

Cub Scouting's 12 Core Values

1. Citizenship
2. Compassion
3. Cooperation
4. Courage
5. Faith
6. Health and Fitness
7. Honesty
8. Perseverance
9. Positive Attitude
10. Resourcefulness
11. Respect
12. Responsibility

Welcome to Tiger Cubs!

(For you and your Tiger Cub to read together.)

We will be doing many exciting things this year with the Tiger Cub den and Cub Scout pack. And some things you will do at home with your family.

The Tiger Cub program is based on the idea of *Search, discover, and share.* That is what you will be doing this year in Tiger Cubs. You will *search* out new activities, *discover* new things, and *share* them with others.

At the first few Tiger Cub den meetings you will be completing the requirements for the Bobcat badge and working on den activities and electives you can count towards your Tiger Cub badge. You will work on your Wolf badge next year, when you are in a Wolf den.

Your adult partner will help you along the steps of the Bobcat trail. When the three specified Bobcat requirements have been completed, you will be awarded the Tiger Cub Immediate Recognition emblem. Once you finish all of the requirements, you will be awarded your Bobcat badge at a pack meeting. You will wear the badge in the appropriate location on the left pocket of your uniform shirt.

When you do things with your Tiger Cub den, you will be wearing your Tiger Cub uniform. Look at the picture on page 7 of this handbook. Can you see something on the Tiger Cub's right shirt pocket? That is called a *Tiger Cub Immediate Recognition Emblem.* You will earn an Immediate Recognition Emblem to wear after you do three things: learn the Cub Scout motto, learn the Cub Scout sign, and learn the Cub Scout salute. As you do these three things, you can color in the tiger paw prints on pages 161 and 162.

As we do fun things with the den and our family this year, you will earn *beads* to put on your emblem. This handbook tells about the different things, called *achievements,* that you can do to earn the beads. You will get a white bead each time you do one of the activities with your family, an orange bead when you do an activity with your den, and a black bead when you go on an outing or field trip, called a *Go See It.* The Tiger Cub Badge Trail on page 163 also has places where you can color in a tiger paw print to mark the achievements you have done. When you have five beads of each color, you will have earned the Tiger Cub rank and will be presented your *Tiger Cub badge* at the next pack meeting.

This handbook also has other things you can do, called *electives*. You and I can do electives any time while you are a Tiger Cub. After we have worked together on 10 electives, and you have earned your Tiger Cub rank, you will receive a *Tiger Track bead* to put on your Tiger Cub Immediate Recognition Emblem. You may earn as many Tiger Track beads as you want to.

In the back of this book, you will find another chart where you can keep track of the electives you do by coloring in a tiger paw print for each activity (see the Tiger Cub Badge Trail on page 163).

We will also go to a Cub Scout *pack meeting* each month. Pack meetings are lots of fun! Your whole family can come along with you and join in the fun.

Tiger Cubs is a very special program, and YOU are a very special boy. Have a great Tiger Cub year!

Welcome to Tiger Cubs!

The Bobcat Badge

The Trail to Bobcat

1 Learn and say the Cub Scout Promise and complete the Honesty Character Connection.

I, [your name], promise to do my best
To do my duty to God and my country,
To help other people, and
To obey the Law of the Pack.

When you say you will do something, that is a **promise**.

Duty to God means that you will put God first and do what you know God wants you to do.

Duty to your country means that you will do what you can for your country. You will be proud that you are an American.

To help other people means that you will do things for other people that will help them.

To obey the Law of the Pack means that you will be a good Cub Scout.

Character Connections®

The Cub Scout Promise—Honesty

Know. What is a promise? What does it mean to keep your word? What does honesty mean? What does it mean to do your best?

Commit. Why is a promise important? Why is it important for people to trust you when you give your word? When might it be difficult to keep your word? Give examples.

Practice. Discuss with family members how honesty is important. How can you do your best to be honest when doing activities in Cub Scouting?

Akela's OK   Date   Recorded by the den leader

2 Say the Law of the Pack. Tell what it means.

The Cub Scout follows Akela.
The Cub Scout helps the pack go.
The pack helps the Cub Scout grow.
The Cub Scout gives goodwill.

Akela (say Ah-KAY-la) means "good leader" to a Cub Scout. Akela is your mother or father. So is your Cubmaster or your den leader. At school, your teacher is Akela.

You say you will **help the pack go.** That means that you will go to your Cub Scout meetings. Do what you can to help. Think of others in the pack.

When you are at your Cub Scout meetings, you will learn new things. You will play games and work with others. This is how **the Cub Scout grows.**

The last part of the Law of the Pack says that you will **give goodwill.** This means that you will always try to smile and be happy. Do things that make other people happy. They don't have to be big things. Little things help, too.

Akela's OK   Date   Recorded by the den leader

3   Tell what Webelos means.

Webelos (say WE-buh-lows) is a Cub Scout secret. Cub Scouts know the secret. It is **WE**'ll **BE LO**yal **S**couts.

Akela's OK   Date   Recorded by the den leader

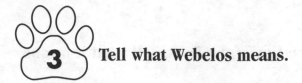

4   Show the Cub Scout sign. Tell what it means.

Make the sign with your right hand. Hold your arm straight up. The two raised fingers stand for two parts of the Cub Scout Promise—"to help other people" and "to obey the Law of the Pack." The two raised fingers look like the sharp ears of the wolf ready to listen to Akela.

Akela's OK   Date   Recorded by the den leader

                                          The Bobcat Badge

5 Show the Cub Scout handshake. Tell what it means.

When you shake hands with
another Cub Scout, do this:
Hold out your right hand just as you always do to
shake hands. But then put your first two fingers along
the inside of the other boy's wrist. This means that
you help and that you obey the Law of the Pack.

Akela's OK   Date   Recorded by the den leader

6 Say the Cub Scout motto. A motto is a guiding principle.

Do Your Best.

A motto is a rule for living. Do your best all the time.
Do your best in school and at home. Do your best
when you play a game and help your team.

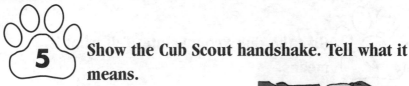

Akela's OK   Date   Recorded by the den leader

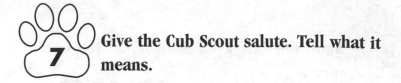

7 Give the Cub Scout salute. Tell what it means.

Salute with your right hand. Hold your first two fingers close together. Touch your fingertips to your cap. If you aren't wearing a cap, touch your right eyebrow. This is the way to show respect to your den leaders. You salute the flag to show respect to our country.

_____ _____ _____
Akela's OK   Date   Recorded by the den leader

8 With your adult partner, complete "A Bobcat Requirement" in front of the Contents pages of this handbook.

_____ _____ _____
Akela's OK   Date   Recorded by the den leader

The Tiger Cub Badge

Achievements

To receive the Tiger Cub rank, the Tiger Cub must complete all 15 parts of the following five achievements with you, his adult partner. You will approve each part after your boy does his best to finish it and sign where it says "Akela's OK."

> Remember that there are no performance requirements for a boy. Simply participating and doing one's best in an activity constitutes completion.

1 Making My Family Special

Making My
Family Special

The people who live with us are called our *family*. Most of us also have family members who live in other places. Every family is different, and every family is special. These activities will help you to learn more about your family.

Note to Adult Partner: The goal of these activities is to make family bonds stronger. Take advantage of opportunities to talk with your Tiger Cub about things that strengthen his family. Reinforce your family values with him, and remind him that he is a very important part of his family!

1F. Family Activity

Everyone in a family is expected to do certain things as part of being a member of that family. Some of these things may be for your own well-being, and some may be to help others. You may be responsible for keeping your bedroom or play area neat and clean. You may also help the family by doing chores such as clearing the table after a meal or taking out the trash. You will find that being dependable can be fun and that you feel good after you get your job done.

REQUIREMENT **1F** **Think of one chore you can do with your adult partner. Complete it together.**

 ## Character Connections®
Making My Family Special—
Responsibility

Know. Think about the job that you completed. What was the hardest part of doing the job? How well was the job done? What does it mean to be responsible?

Commit. Why is being responsible important? Are there jobs you can do by yourself? List other ways that you can be responsible.

Practice. Do requirement 1F.

Note to Adult Partner: This activity can help a boy learn that every family member has a part in keeping a home clean, tidy, and in good repair. Doing chores together promotes family understanding and togetherness and can provide good opportunities to talk, as well as to teach skills. You can do this activity with the Tiger Cub or with the whole family.

The chore you choose to do together should not take too long or be too difficult or unpleasant.

In addition to stressing responsibility, this activity reinforces the fact that caring for one's home and belongings can be enjoyable and that it makes us feel good about ourselves. It also shows the Tiger Cub that having a positive attitude can make work more enjoyable.

Did You Know?...that Cub Scout leaders have responsibilities? One of your Tiger Cub den leader's responsibilities is to attend the pack leaders' meeting each month. At this meeting, leaders plan the den and pack program and manage the affairs of the pack.

1D. Den Activity

Every Tiger Cub has special family memories. Maybe you remember a family birthday party or a family vacation. Special memories are often simple things, like a time when you had a lot of fun playing a game with your family or putting something together. Keeping a scrapbook is a way to remember those special times.

After you make a family scrapbook with your den, have your adult partner help you to think of things you can keep in it.

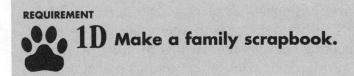
Materials: Three-prong folder for each boy; three-hole-punched copy or construction paper; markers, crayons, stickers and other materials to decorate the cover

Boys decorate the folder as desired and then fasten the paper into it.

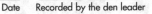

Note to Adult Partner: Memories of special times he has had with his loved ones help to reinforce the bond a Tiger Cub feels with his family. Encourage your Tiger Cub to add things to his scrapbook throughout the year: photographs, pictures he has drawn, ticket stubs or brochures from places he has visited, gift tags, holiday cards, postcards, programs from special events—or even a leaf as a memory of a day that he raked leaves and jumped into the leaf pile. Also encourage him to keep the scrapbook where other family members can look at it from time to time. When they do, their enjoyment will make him feel special!

The above directions for a scrapbook are only a suggestion. The boy–adult partner team leading this activity may have different ideas for making a scrapbook.

Note: If you use recycled or inexpensive materials for your scrapbook, you will be teaching your Tiger Cub to be *resourceful,* which is one of Cub Scouting's 12 core values.

Did You Know?...that Cub Scout packs all over the United States create a special memory each February? They have a *blue and gold banquet* to celebrate the founding of the Boy Scouts of America in 1910 and of Cub Scouting in 1930. The second week in February is Scouting Anniversary Week, which includes the day that the Boy Scouts of America was incorporated on February 8, 1910.

1G. Go See It!

In some ways, family life was different many years ago. But there were some things that were the same, too. It is interesting to see how people lived years ago.

Akela's OK   Date   Recorded by the den leader

Note to Adult Partner: This Go See It offers an opportunity for Tiger Cubs to show *respect,* which is one of Cub Scouting's 12 core values. If boys visit a historical building or museum, for instance, they will need to show respect by behaving well. If they visit an older person, they will be showing respect for their elders by being attentive and polite.

After completing this Go See It, it would be fun to share with your Tiger Cub what your family life was like when *you* were in first grade. Encourage him to ask his grandparents or other older family members what their families were like, too.

Did You Know?... that Tiger Cubs, BSA, was started in 1982 as a program for boy–adult partner teams with shared leadership? Today, Tiger Cubs is a family- and home-centered program that encourages ethical decision-making skills for first-grade (or 7-year-old) boys. The program emphasizes shared leadership, learning about the community, and family understanding.

2 Where I live

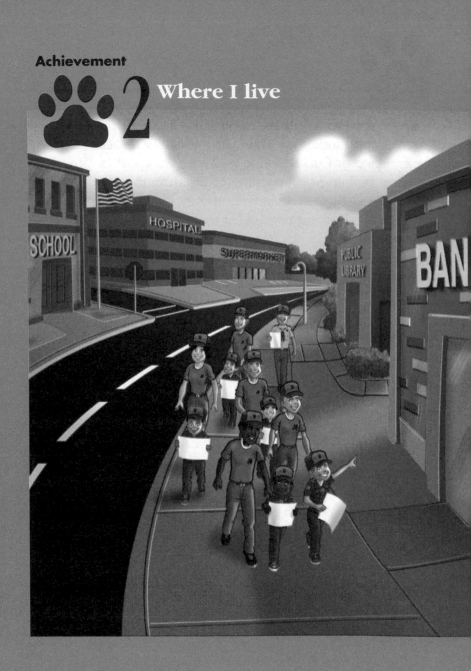

Where I live

Some people live in big cities. Some live in small cities or towns. The nearest neighbors of some people live miles away on a farm, and some, in an apartment right next door. Wherever you live, the buildings and homes around you and the people who live, work, and play near you are called your *community*.

It is important to learn about your community. Communities are stronger when the people who live in them take care of them and are good neighbors to each other. As you learn more about your community, you will be more proud of it and become a better citizen.

Note to Adult Partner: One of the purposes of Cub Scouting and aims of Scouting, as well as one of the 12 core values of Cub Scouting, is to develop responsible *citizenship* in boys. This begins with an understanding of their community. As you explore your community with your Tiger Cub and his den, the boys will develop a deeper appreciation of their community and what it means to be a part of it.

2F. Family Activity

Maps help us find new places, and maps help us find our way home if we are lost. Have you ever looked at a map of your neighborhood?

 2F **Look at a map of your community with your adult partner.**

The map can be one your adult partner has, or it can be a map that you and your adult partner draw together. On that map, find or mark your home, and find or mark three places you like to go to. Places to find on the map could be your school, the place where you worship, the place where you have your pack meetings, a store, a park or playground, or the house of a friend or relative.

Note to Adult Partner: As you help your Tiger Cub find familiar places on a map, point out the names of the streets. When you take short trips, such as to the grocery store, encourage your Tiger Cub to be the navigator and use a map. You can incorporate map reading into other family activities, helping your Tiger Cub become a better map reader. Keep these activities simple, and involve the whole family if you can. It is better for him to be able to find familiar places on the map by himself. As his map-reading skills develop, this will become a useful resource for him. *Resourcefulness* is one of the 12 core values of Cub Scouting.

Did You Know?...that there are more than 2 million Cub Scouts in the United States? It would take a very big map to include all their homes!

2D. Den Activity

When we say the Pledge of Allegiance, we show that we are proud to live in our country. If you are wearing your Tiger Cub uniform when you say the Pledge of Allegiance, give the Cub Scout salute and face the U.S. flag. You do not have to take off your Tiger Cub cap if you are wearing one. If you say the Pledge of Allegiance when you are not in uniform, remove your hat if you are wearing one, and place your right hand over your heart. When you salute or place your hand over your heart, you are showing your respect for the flag.

REQUIREMENT
2D **Practice the Pledge of Allegiance with your den, and participate in a den or pack flag ceremony.**

I pledge allegiance to the flag of the United States of America and to the Republic for which it stands, one nation under God, indivisible, with liberty and justice for all.

Character Connections®
Where I Live—Citizenship

Know. What does it mean to be a good citizen? Why do you think we say the Pledge of Allegiance?

Commit. Is it easy to be a good citizen? Why is it important to show respect to the flag even if others around you might not?

Practice. Do requirement 2D.

_____   _____
Akela's OK   Date   Recorded by the den leader

Note to Adult Partner: If Tiger Cubs say the Pledge of Allegiance with the audience during an opening ceremony at a pack meeting, that is considered participation in this requirement. This requirement can also be accomplished by having a flag ceremony during the Tiger Cub den meeting. Tiger Cub dens are encouraged to have their own U.S. flag and to open each den meeting with the Pledge of Allegiance. The boys don't have to have the pledge memorized. At the beginning of the year, have boys say it in a "repeat-after-me" fashion. (Note that "one nation under God" is spoken as a continuous phrase, with no pause between "nation" and "under.")

Did You Know?...that special ribbons and awards, such as the National Den Award, may be attached to the top of your den flag? The boys enjoy watching the ribbons accumulate.

2G. Go See It!

Every community has many people who help you if you are hurt or in trouble. There are also people who help during emergencies, such as a fire or a bad storm. Many of these people teach us how to help keep accidents from happening and teach us what we should do if there is an emergency. Two kinds of community helpers are police officers and firefighters.

REQUIREMENT 2G Visit a police station or fire station. Ask someone who works there how he or she helps people in your community.

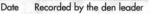

Note to Adult Partner: For this activity, you can visit any emergency response facility, such as a police station or sheriff's office, fire station or volunteer fire department, or search-and-rescue team. The purpose of this activity is to have the boys learn that people work in the community to protect them and keep them safe.

You could ask your Tiger Cub what he thinks would happen if we didn't have any police officers or firefighters. You could also talk with him about the courage various community helpers show as they do their jobs. *Courage* is one of Cub Scouting's 12 core values.

When you talk to emergency workers, ask them to tell the boys about the training they had for their jobs. Ask them what they like about their jobs. Most police officers and firefighters welcome visits from children. But be prepared to change your plans if an emergency takes them away shortly before or during your visit.

Did You Know?...that BSA has a publication called *Guide to Safe Scouting* that includes important guidelines for conducting safe Scouting activities? You can also access it through the BSA's official Web site:

http://www.scouting.org/healthandsafety

Achievement 3

Keeping Myself Healthy and Safe

Keeping Myself Healthy and Safe

Staying healthy and safe includes many things. To be as healthy as we can be, it is important to eat good foods, get plenty of sleep, and exercise to keep our bodies strong. We also need to keep our bodies clean and brush our teeth regularly. To be safe, it is important to understand what to do in case of emergencies, and to follow the rules we are taught about how to act when we feel uncomfortable with someone.

Note to Adult Partner: *Health and fitness* are included in the 12 core values of Cub Scouting. Scouting programs for youth of all ages are designed to promote physical, mental, and emotional fitness. Talk with your Tiger Cub about developing lifetime habits that will keep him healthy, and share with him how important it is to you that he is healthy and safe. It is important to tell him what to do when he is around a stranger or another person who makes him feel uncomfortable. The Youth Protection information in the beginning of this handbook—"How to Protect Your Children from Child Abuse"—can help you with some of these topics.

3F. Family Activity

Knowing what to do when there is an emergency is very important. One type of an emergency would be a fire in your home. Another would be if you became lost or separated from an adult while you were away from home.

A. You have probably had a fire drill at your school. But what about at home?

B. Have you ever felt lost? Sometimes, when you become separated from the people you are with, you are not really very far away from them, but you may feel very alone. You need to know what to do when you are lost or separated.

REQUIREMENT

3Fa **With your family, plan a fire drill and then practice it in your home.**

Be sure to plan a safe meeting place outside that everyone can go to. That way, you will know everyone is safe. Go to that safe place as part of your practice.

REQUIREMENT

3Fb **With your adult partner, plan what to do if you became lost or separated from your family in a strange place.**

Then practice what you would do with your adult partner if that happened. By practicing, you will learn that you are being brave when you stay where you are. You will be found faster, too!

Akela's OK   Date   Recorded by the den leader

Note to Adult Partner: A. Contact your local fire department for information on planning a fire drill in your home. Fire departments often have special activities during October, which is Fire Safety Month. It's a good idea to have regular fire drills with your family to reinforce your family emergency plan.

B. Tell your Tiger Cub that if he ever feels that he is lost, he should stay where he is and hold on to something such as a bench, a post, or a tree. (This will make him feel more secure.) Explain to him that he is showing *courage,* one of the 12 core values of Cub Scouting, when he stays in one place, even though he might want to try to find you. Assure him that because you love him, you will begin looking for him as soon as you realize he is missing. Explain to him that if he moves around, it will take you longer to find him.

In a safe place, practice a game with him where he pretends that he is lost and holds on to something stationary. Walk out of sight and return three to five minutes later. It would be good to practice this a few times a year while he is young.

Did You Know?...that a Cub Scout pack is required to follow the safety rules set for the meeting place it is using? For instance, if you meet in a school, a religious institution, or other public building, be sure to check the fire regulations before using lit candles. (And also check with the owner of the facility!)

3D. Den Activity

To keep your body healthy, it is important that you eat a well-balanced diet. The Food Guide Pyramid helps you by showing foods you should have each day.

MyPyramid.gov
STEPS TO A HEALTHIER YOU

Did You Know?... You can get a food plan designed *just for you*—on the Internet, go to www.mypyramid.gov. You just enter your age, choose "male" or "female," and choose your usual level of physical activity, and you'll get a plan of what and how much you should eat. You'll also get lots of tips to help you make wise meal and snack choices.

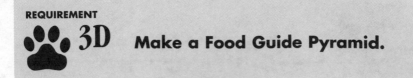

3D   Make a Food Guide Pyramid.

Have your adult partner draw a Food Guide Pyramid on a big piece of paper or posterboard. Cut out pictures of food from old magazines and glue them in the right places on the pyramid. You could also draw pictures of different foods on your Food Guide Pyramid. You could display your Food Guide Pyramid at the next pack meeting.

Character Connections®
Keeping Myself Healthy and Safe—
Health and Fitness

Know. With a family adult, have a healthy snack.

Commit. When is it difficult to eat healthy food?

Practice. What foods are best for your health and growth?

Akela's OK		Date	Recorded by the den leader

Note to Adult Partner: Food magazines and grocery store advertisements in newspapers are good sources for pictures of food. Den families could donate old magazines. This activity will be a better learning experience for the den if they have a lot of pictures available to use.

In the days after this den activity, you might want to take the opportunity to discuss food choices with your Tiger Cub. Remember that it is better to praise him for making good choices than to scold him for making poor choices.

Did You Know?...that the BSA encourages Cub Scout packs to participate in community service activities. Some packs collect food for local food banks or clothing for shelters. Others help clean up local parks, or do special service projects for their chartered organizations.

3G. Go See It!

It is fun to play games and to take part in sports. It is also good exercise, which helps to keep your body healthy. Some games and sports are for one person, and sometimes people play games or sports on teams. You will have fun watching other people play games or showing what they can do. Understanding the rules of the game or sport you are watching makes it a lot more fun.

REQUIREMENT

3G

Learn the rules of a game or sport. Then, go watch an amateur or professional game or sporting event.

Akela's OK | Date | Recorded by the den leader

Note to Adult Partner: If you live in an area where a professional sporting team plays, watching one of their games could be exciting for the whole den. Some local recreation departments and high schools have sporting events that are open to the public. Many of these local events are free or don't cost as much as professional games, and they may have shorter playing time, which could be a plus for Tiger Cub-age boys. Tiger Cubs would have fun watching a swimming meet, bowling competition, or gymnastics events, as well as baseball, basketball, soccer, and other sports.

Let the Tiger Cubs help to decide where they will go. You may encourage them to choose to go to a game or sporting event that they have not seen before. While you are there, point out examples of *good sportsmanship*—one of the purposes of Cub Scouting—and tell boys that it is important that all players try to do their best—even if they don't win.

You can point out several of Cub Scouting's 12 core values while watching a sporting event. Players of a team sport show *cooperation*, and they must be *physically fit* to compete. You could also point out that it takes *perseverance* and a great deal of practice to develop a skill.

Did You Know?...that Cub Scouting has a supplemental enrichment program called Cub Scout Academics and Sports? See pages 153–156 and check with your pack leaders to learn more about the requirements and what your Tiger Cub can do to take part.

How I Tell It

When we talk with people, we communicate information to them about something we want them to know. We also communicate when we write, draw, sing, dance, or show pictures. We can communicate using our bodies or faces, too, such as when we smile or frown. When you raise your hand in school, you are communicating to your teacher that you want to talk. The number of beads on your Tiger Cub Immediate Recognition Emblem communicates to people how many Tiger Cub achievement parts you have completed. People also communicate with telephones and computers and through television, radio, newspapers, magazines, and books.

Note to Adult Partner: Good communication skills are important for people of all ages. These activities are designed to make learning about communication fun and interesting.

4F. Family Activity

Mealtime can be a good time to talk with your family members. You can share things with your family, and you can also listen to them while they share with you.

REQUIREMENT 4F

At a family meal, have each family member take turns telling the others one thing that happened to him or her that day. Remember to practice being a good listener while you wait for your turn to talk.

Character Connections®
How I Tell It—Respect

Know. When talking with other family members, how do you show courtesy and respect? How do you listen respectfully? How can you interrupt people and still be respectful?

Commit. How does it feel when people listen to you with respect? List three things to remember that will help you talk respectfully with others.

Practice. Join in a family conversation. After the conversation, discuss how you and others showed respect.

_____   _____
Akela's OK   Date   Recorded by the den leader

Note to Adult Partner: Mealtimes are not the best time to have unpleasant conversations or to discuss angry feelings. Try to keep mealtime conversations positive. Sharing about your day at a mealtime can become a regular family activity. For this activity, try to choose a mealtime when most or all family members are there. Sharing among family members is always good— even if only two members of the family are eating together. Make sure each person has an opportunity to speak without interruptions or negative comments.

This is a good opportunity for you to teach your Tiger Cub and other children in the family to be polite and to be good listeners. If someone in the family shares a sad or difficult experience, set an example for your Tiger Cub by showing *compassion*, which is one of Cub Scouting's 12 core values.

Did You Know?...that *family understanding* is one of the 10 purposes of Cub Scouting? (You can review the 10 purposes of Cub Scouting on page 21.)

4D. Den Activity

When we talk with other people, we want them to understand what we are telling them. Sometimes when people tell a story, they may forget a part of it or change something just a little. Even if they do not mean for it to happen, the story can change a lot if it is told several times. This game is a fun way to show how a story can change when it is told many times.

Achievements

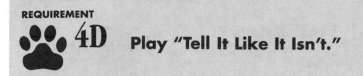

4D   Play "Tell It Like It Isn't."

To play this game, Tiger Cubs form a line. The first Tiger Cub whispers one sentence to the second Tiger Cub. Each one takes his turn, whispering the sentence to the next boy. The last boy repeats the sentence out loud. How close is it to the original sentence? Take turns and play a few more times. The boys will have even more fun if adult partners join in the game, too!

_____   _____ _____
Akela's OK   Date   Recorded by the den leader

Note to Adult Partner: This game is a good opportunity to teach your Tiger Cub that when someone tells him something, it may not always be accurate. A message can change when repeated often, even if people don't mean it to. Gossip and unkind words can do a lot of harm and are often untrue. Remind Tiger Cubs that they should always try to say only things that are true. *Honesty* is one of Cub Scouting's 12 core values.

Did You Know?... that the Boy Scouts of America communicates to leaders through lots of publications, and videos, too? A Cub Scout leader roundtable is a monthly supplemental training for Cub Scout leaders in your district.

It provides program ideas, policy guidelines, and information on events in your district and council. Check with your pack leaders for the time and place of your district roundtable.

2006–2007 CUB SCOUT ROUNDTABLE PLANNING GUIDE

4G. Go See It!

When people want to communicate with hundreds or thousands of people at the same time, they may use a television or radio broadcast, or they may write their message in a newspaper, book, or magazine.

REQUIREMENT 4G

Visit a television station, radio station, or newspaper office. Find out how people there communicate to others.

Note to Adult Partner: If your community doesn't have opportunities for you to take the den to visit a television station, radio station, or newspaper office, you may take them to a print shop, copy center, or business that reproduces its own newsletter. Your school or place of worship may have equipment for reproducing fliers and newsletters. The goal is to show boys how media can be used to communicate with a lot of people. One benefit of visiting a television station, radio station, or newspaper office is that boys may be reminded of the visit when watching television, listening to the radio, or reading a newspaper.

Did You Know?...that the Boy Scouts of America publishes *Boys' Life* magazine for youth and *Scouting* magazine for adult leaders? There is even a version of *Boys' Life* published especially for Tiger Cub– and Cub Scout–age boys.

Achievement

5 Let's Go Outdoors

Let's Go Outdoors

There is so much to do and learn outdoors! You can have fun exploring nature and looking at trees, flowers, and animals. You can walk, run, play games, and ride a bike. It is even fun to just sit outside and pay attention to all the things going on around you!

Completing one part of this achievement will help you earn the Cub Scout Outdoor Activity Award. (See page 149.) Completing this achievement is required to earn Cub Scouting's Leave No Trace Awareness Award. (See page 151.)

Note to Adult Partner: The goal of these activities is to develop in your Tiger Cub an appreciation of and awe and respect for the world around him. It may also provide a basis for hobbies and interests that he might pursue for the rest of his life. This offers you an opportunity to reinforce your own values about the environment and our place in it.

5F. Family Activity

You can listen to a weather report on the radio or television. But it is more fun to watch the weather for yourself by going outside and using your five senses: seeing, hearing, smelling, tasting, and touching.

Some people cannot use all five senses fully, such as people who are sight-impaired or hearing-impaired. Often, people who cannot use one or more of their senses have learned to use the other senses very well.

REQUIREMENT

5F **Go outside and watch the weather.**

Use your senses to help you describe what the weather is like. What does the temperature *feel* like? Can you *feel* wind on your face? What do you *see?* — Is it dark or sunny? Are there clouds in the sky? Can you *smell* a storm coming? Do you *hear* thunder or rain? Can you *taste* dust that has blown into your mouth?

Character Connections®
Let's Go Outdoors—Faith

Know. Discuss things about the weather that you know to be true, but you cannot see at the moment, such as is the sun still there although you only see clouds? Is the moon there, even though it is day? Can you see wind? Do you know that the rain will eventually stop? Do you have faith in other things you can't see?

Commit. What makes it difficult to believe in things that you cannot see? What helps you to develop faith?

Practice. Do requirement 5F.

Akela's OK _____ Date _____ Recorded by the den leader

Note to Adult Partner: This is a simple activity, but it can be a lot of fun for the whole family. You may just step outside to observe the weather, or you may want to take a walk. For a little extra fun, your Tiger Cub may want to pretend to be a weather reporter and "report" the weather to the family.

Did You Know?...that *spiritual growth* is one of the 10 purposes of Cub Scouting? (You can review the purposes of Cub Scouting on page 21.) Every level of Scouting encourages a boy to explore the faith of his family. Ask your religious leader or local council service center about the religious emblems programs available to Tiger Cubs.

5D. Den Activity

Many trees and bushes have leaves that turn colors and fall to the ground in the fall. Some trees have needles that stay on all year long. You may live in a place where cacti grow. Cacti have spines or scales instead of leaves. Go outdoors with your adult partner and collect some leaves to take to your den meeting for this activity. Be sure to collect only leaves that have fallen off a tree or bush, or get the permission of an adult before removing a live part of a tree or bush.

5D **With a crayon or colored pencil and a piece of paper, make a leaf rubbing.**

Materials: Writing paper, leaves, crayons

Put a leaf, vein side up, on a smooth surface, and cover it with a piece of thin writing paper. Hold the paper firmly in position and gently rub the crayon over it. The crayon strokes should all be in the same direction, with just enough pressure to bring out the details of the leaf. You can decorate or frame your finished design and display it in your home. You can also make your leaf rubbings into greeting cards or give them away as a gift.

(1) SILVER MAPLE
(2) AMERICAN ELM
(3) MAGNOLIA
(4) WHITE OAK
(5) HORSE CHESTNUT
(6) ASPEN
(7) WHITE MULBERRY
(8) BLACK WILLOW

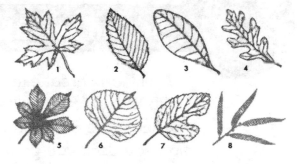

Akela's OK   Date   Recorded by the den leader

Note to Adult Partner: This is a good activity for autumn, when leaves are falling. If you live in an area that doesn't have deciduous trees, or if you want to do this activity in the winter, you can use pine needles or other evergreen foliage. While your Tiger Cub is coloring, you could ask him whether he can remember what the trees look like at different times of the year. You could also ask him whether he can think of any animals that live in or under trees.

Did You Know?...that next year, when your Tiger Cub is in a Wolf Cub Scout den, he can earn the Cub Scout World Conservation Award? This award emphasizes the importance of our natural resources and our interdependence with other countries in our world environment.

5G. Go See It!

Walking is great exercise, and it is fun to be outdoors. When you walk, you see more things in the outdoors than you do if you go fast on a bicycle or in a car or bus.

Your den may go to a special outdoor place for a hike or take a simple walk in the neighborhood. Wherever you go, it is fun to be outdoors!

_____ _____ _____
Akela's OK   Date   Recorded by the den leader

Note to Adult Partner: You can take the boys to a park, along a nature trail, into the woods or forest, to a neighboring city, or around a high school or college grounds. If possible, take the boys to a special location or a place they have not been to before. Many nature parks will have someone to guide you on your hike. You may want to have a picnic or a snack break on your hike. Even if you stay in your neighborhood, the boys will enjoy their time outdoors.

Keep your hike short enough so that all the boys will enjoy it, and be certain that the boys wear shoes and clothing appropriate for the hike. Be sure to take enough drinking water for everyone, for both during and after the hike. If the boys become too tired or are uncomfortable, they probably will not have a pleasant memory of this Go See It.

Did You Know?...that Cub Scout day camp is an organized one- to five-day camping program for Cub Scouts and Webelos Scouts? Day camp is held under certified leadership at an approved site during daylight and/or early evening hours. Check with your den leader to see whether your district or council has a day camp program.

Electives

Once a boy has earned his Tiger Cub badge, he can earn Tiger Track beads. For each 10 electives he finishes, the Tiger Cub will receive one Tiger Track bead. The Tiger Cub is not expected to complete all of the electives. There are many choices and a wide variety of activities. Many of the electives offer several things that a boy can do to receive credit for completion.

Boys may do electives more than once and count them toward a Tiger Track bead each time they are completed.

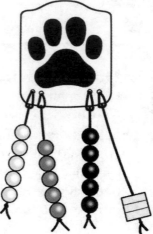

A Tiger Cub may complete electives while working on achievements, but he can't receive a Tiger Track bead until after he has earned his Tiger Cub badge.

1

How Do You Celebrate?

Celebrating is a way of making an event or occasion special. Families celebrate different kinds of things in different ways. Many families celebrate religious holidays, cultural holidays, national holidays, birthdays, anniversaries, and special events. Families can also celebrate good news, successful days at work or school, the arrival of a new pet, the first snow, the change of season, moving to a new home, or a visit from someone they have not seen in a long time.

Think of a time when your family celebrated something, and then tell the den about it and how it made you feel.

You can draw or bring a picture or some other items to your den meeting to show. See how many different kinds of celebrations everyone in your den can think of!

1   Akela's OK   Date   Recorded by the den leader

Note to Adult Partner: Allow your Tiger Cub to share as much as he can with his den. If he needs help, prompt him with some memories. If he is uncomfortable talking to den members, help him, but don't take the attention away from him. Cub Scouting offers many opportunities for boys to become comfortable speaking to others in a relaxed environment with friends. This will help them build self-confidence.

For this activity, you and your Tiger Cub might find it helpful to draw a picture of the celebration, or just write the name of the celebration on a piece of sturdy paper. On the other side of the paper, you can help him write notes or draw pictures to remind him of the things he wants to tell the den. He can show the den the picture as he looks at the notes or pictures he has made for himself.

Making Decorations

Every day is special, but some days are extra special. Sometimes we decorate things to show how extra special they are. We see decorations at holiday times. Sometimes we decorate for a change of season. It is fun to make decorations for ourselves and for others.

Make a decoration with your family or your den. Display it or give it to someone as a gift.

Balloon Bouquet

Balloons are great decorations for almost any occasion. Try making a balloon bouquet for a birthday.

Materials: Balloons; dowels or sticks; metal can; gift wrap, newspaper comics, or any brightly colored paper; stones or sand

Blow up five to seven balloons and attach them to balloon sticks or tape them to dowels. Cover an empty can with paper. Tape the paper securely around the can. Insert the balloons into the can, and you have your bouquet! Place stones or sand in the can to keep the balloon bouquet from tipping over.

Snowflakes

It is fun to make snowflakes in the wintertime, even if you don't have any snow where you live. Your snowflakes will be different from the ones the other Tiger Cubs make— just like in nature, where no two snowflakes are alike!

Fold a square piece of paper as shown in 1, 2, 3, and 4 below. Then cut as shown in 4. Before unfolding, make more cuts in the sides as shown in 5 or in your own pattern. Unfold and see what kind of snowflake you made!

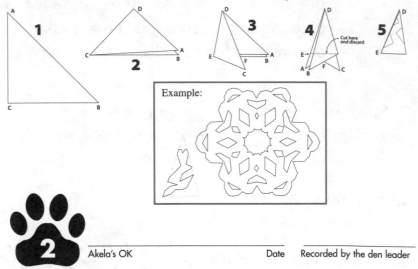

Example:

Akela's OK   Date   Recorded by the den leader

Note to Adult Partner: You can help your Tiger Cub make one of the decorations here, or use any other idea you or another den member may have. You can also check in the children's section of your local library for decoration ideas. Boys are proud when their handiwork is displayed. This would also be a good activity for den members to make gifts for family or friends at a holiday time or for you to make something special together with your Tiger Cub to give to another family member. This way, your Tiger Cub can learn about the joy of giving to others.

Fun and Games

It is fun to play games and do puzzles. When we play with others, it is even more fun!

With your family, play a card game or board game or put a jigsaw puzzle together.

3 Akela's OK _____ Date Recorded by the den leader

Note to Adult Partner: Playing together with family members is time well-spent. When the Tiger Cub plays with his family, he learns that other members of the family enjoy spending time with him. It also draws families together and creates a relaxing atmosphere. Playing games offers you the opportunity to reinforce the importance of taking turns, playing fairly, and being a good sport. Assembling jigsaw puzzles helps your Tiger Cub practice his spatial and fine motor skills. All this, and *fun*, too!

Display a Picture

It is nice to have pictures of your family on display—especially when some of your family members are not close by all the time.

Make a frame for a family picture.

Glue tongue depressors or craft sticks together in a shape to fit your picture. If you like, you can decorate your frame using buttons, shells, small toys, crayons—anything you can think of! Attach a string or ribbon to the upper corners to use as a hanger. Tape your picture to the back of the frame and display it. You can use a photograph or a picture that you draw of your family.

4

Note to Adult Partner: Boys love to see pictures of themselves, especially pictures of themselves when they were younger because it shows them how much they have grown. Remind your Tiger Cub that the picture—and therefore your family—would not be the same without him.

Family Mobile

Each member of your family is special in some way. They all have different hobbies and abilities. Someone may like airplanes. Another may play basketball. And someone else may like gardening or reading. Think of one special thing that reminds you of each member of your family. You can also include grandparents, uncles, and aunts if you want to. And remember to include yourself and family pets!

Make a family mobile.

Materials: Lightweight wire coat hanger, clay, scraps of cloth, rocks, construction paper, heavy sewing thread, felt-tip markers

Begin the mobile by opening up and straightening out a wire coat hanger. Using pliers, adult partners should bend it to form the shape shown. Make a base out of rocks covered with clay and push one end of the hanger into it. Draw pictures of the things that remind you of your family members, or make small models of them out of paper, cloth, or clay. Hang each mobile piece from the wire with a piece of thread.

5

_____   ____   _____
Akela's OK   Date   Recorded by the den leader

Note to Adult Partner: Have a lot of different materials and scraps available for boys to use to make their mobiles. This will inspire their creativity. Allow your boy to choose his own mobile shapes for each member of the family. You may be surprised to see what he chooses to represent each family member!

Song Time

6

Most people enjoy singing together with others. It is fun to sing! Your den could volunteer to sing a song at the next pack meeting.

Along with your adult partner, teach a song to your family or to your den and sing it together.

"I've Got That Tiger Cub Spirit"

(*Tune:* "I've Got That Cub Scout Spirit")

The singers can point to each part of the body mentioned in the verses as they sing.

I've got that Tiger Cub spirit up in my head,
Up in my head, up in my head.
I've got that Tiger Cub spirit up in my head,
Up in my head to stay.

Second Verse
I've got that Tiger Cub spirit deep in my heart,
Deep in my heart, deep in my heart.
I've got that Tiger Cub spirit deep in my heart,
Deep in my heart to stay.

Third Verse
...down in my feet...

Fourth Verse
...all over me...

Fifth Verse

I've got that Tiger Cub spirit up in my head,
Deep in my heart, down in my feet.
I've got that Tiger Cub spirit all over me,
All over me to stay.

"If You're a Tiger and You Know It"

(*Tune:* "If You're Happy and You Know It")

Boys extend and curl their fingers like claws.
If you're a Tiger and you know it, show your claws.
If you're a Tiger and you know it, show your claws.
If you're a Tiger and you know it, then your claws will
surely show it.
If you're a Tiger and you know it, show your claws.

Boys stand up tall and straight.
If you're a Tiger and you know it, show you're strong.
If you're a Tiger and you know it, show you're strong.
If you're a Tiger and you know it, then your strength will
surely show it.
If you're a Tiger and you know it, show you're strong.

Boys make a loud roaring sound.
If you're a Tiger and you know it, give a roar.
If you're a Tiger and you know it, give a roar.
If you're a Tiger and you know it, then your roar will
surely show it.
If you're a Tiger and you know it, give a roar.

Boys perform motions for each line.
If you're a Tiger and you know it, show all three.
If you're a Tiger and you know it, show all three.
If you're a Tiger and you know it, then you really want to
show it,
If you're a Tiger and you know it, show all three.

Note to Adult Partner: Songs with motions can help release Tiger Cub energy. Encourage the boys to teach or take turns leading songs, but be there beside them to prompt them if they need help. You can find more songs in *Cub Scout Program Helps* and the *Cub Scout Songbook.*

ELECTIVE 7
Play Along!

Musical instruments are wonderful, from flutes and chimes to the big bass drum. Maybe you know someone who plays an instrument—maybe the piano or a violin. Did you know that *you* can play a musical instrument? Sure you can! Make one of these, and then have fun playing it.

Make a musical instrument and play it with others. The others can sing or have instruments of their own.

Pie Pan Tambourine

Materials: Aluminum foil pie pans; dried beans, rice, or gravel; stapler; crepe paper

Put the beans, rice, or gravel in one pan. Put the other pan on top and staple the rims together. Attach some crepe paper streamers, and it will look as good as it sounds.

Paper Flute

Materials: Cardboard tube from paper towels or kitchen wrap, waxed paper, rubber band, sharp point (such as an ice pick, awl, or small nail)

Cut a circle of waxed paper about 5 inches in diameter. Fold the waxed paper over the end of the cardboard tube and hold it in place by wrapping a rubber band around it. Have your adult partner help you punch holes down the side of the tube, 1 inch apart. Whistle, sing, or blow into the open end of the flute while covering various combinations of holes for different tones.

Soda Straw Oboe

Materials: Large soda straw, scissors

Flatten one end of a large soda straw about ¾ inch from the end. Cut off both corners of the flattened end diagonally. Blow gently through the flattened end. To make a higher note, trim the other end of the straw. The more you cut off, the higher the note will be.

Akela's OK   Date   Recorded by the den leader

Note to Adult Partner: Why not make your own instrument and join in the band?

Your Religious Leaders

Get to know the people who lead and teach at your place of worship.

Invite a religious leader or teacher from your place of worship to your home or to your den meeting.

Akela's OK   Date   Recorded by the den leader

Note to Adult Partner: By inviting one of your religious leaders to your home or den meeting, your Tiger Cub will have the opportunity to get to know him or her better. This would be a good time to talk with your religious leader about the availability of a religious emblem for your faith. You may also invite someone who teaches youth classes at your place of worship, or a religious leader associated with your pack's chartered organization.

A New Friend

When people move to a new place, they have to make new friends and learn about their new neighborhood. It is much easier if friendly Tiger Cubs help them and introduce them to new friends.

Help a new boy or girl get to know other people.

You can do this by inviting him/her to play with you and your friends, by helping him/her find the way at school, or by telling him/her about the community. Maybe you can think of another way to help a new person.

Note to Adult Partner: The new child your Tiger Cub helps may be a boy or a girl. The child may be new to the neighborhood or new to the school, pack, or place of worship. The intent of this elective is to teach your Tiger Cub to reach out to newcomers and to make them feel welcome. Set a good example by doing the same with the new child's parents. This is similar to one of the many enriching family activities that you can find in *Cub Scouting's BSA Family Activity Book*.

ELECTIVE 10 Helping Hands

When people grow older, or if they become sick or have an accident, they sometimes have a hard time doing everyday things. If you know an elderly person or if you know someone who is ill or recovering from an illness or accident, try to think of what things might be hard for them to do by themselves.

Along with your adult partner, help an elderly or shut-in person with a chore.

You might offer to do things such as helping to take out trash, rake leaves, or bring in the mail. Ask first, and do it with a big Tiger Cub smile!

10 Akela's OK   Date   Recorded by the den leader

Note to Adult Partner: This activity helps you teach your Tiger Cub to be considerate of the needs of others and to be helpful. Remind him that when he says the Cub Scout Promise, he promises to "help other people," and praise him for his efforts when he does. Reflect with him on how it feels to help others.

Helping the Needy

Tiger Cubs and Cub Scout packs often help collect food, clothing, and toys for needy families.

Help collect food, clothing, or toys for needy families with your den or pack.

Note to Adult Partner: Many packs participate in organized collections of food, clothing, or toys each year. Reflect with your Tiger Cub about where the items he helped to collect will go and how helping made him feel.

ELECTIVE 12 — A Friendly Greeting

People who are in the hospital or a care facility sometimes feel lonely. A card or a visit from a friendly Tiger Cub can help a lot.

Make at least two cards or decorations and take them to a hospital or long-term care facility.

The card can be like the example shown, or make up your own cheery greeting.

12   Akela's OK   Date   Recorded by the den leader

Note to Adult Partner: Be sure to call before visiting to find out whether visitors are welcome and whether there are visiting hours. Some residents at long-term care facilities love to hear children sing or watch them perform. But hospitals cannot always accept young visitors. In this case, you might go to a hospital and give cards or decorations to a hospital volunteer. Reflect with your Tiger Cub about how the people he visited are being cared for and how his visit made a difference.

13 Making Change

Learning to count coins and to make change accurately takes practice. But it is an important thing to learn to do.

Using U.S. pennies, dimes, nickels, and quarters, choose the correct coins to make the following amounts.

There may be more than one answer. You could see how many answers you can come up with.

15 cents	60 cents
50 cents	35 cents
27 cents	59 cents

Example 1: (15 cents)

Example 2: (15 cents)

If you gave a clerk at a store a one dollar bill for the following purchases, how much change would you get back?

99 cents	25 cents
50 cents	76 cents

Akela's OK   Date   Recorded by the den leader

Note to Adult Partner: This activity will help to build your Tiger Cub's arithmetic skills, as well as his ability to make change. Depending on his skills, he might need some instruction from you to complete this elective. This is a great way to pass time while waiting for your food at a restaurant or for an appointment. As your boy gets better, practice with different denominations of paper bills.

Reading Fun

As a Tiger Cub, you are working hard on learning to read this year in school. The more you practice, the more you will enjoy reading.

Together with your adult partner, read a short story or a magazine article.

14 Akela's OK _____   Date _____   Recorded by the den leader

Note to Adult Partner: Depending on your Tiger Cub's reading skills, he may read to you, or you may do most of the reading. The important thing is to establish a habit of reading together as his reading skills develop. Encourage him to read often, and give him plenty of positive reinforcement as he reads.

Our Colorful World

Believe it or not, all colors are made from just three main colors, called *primary colors*. The primary colors are red, yellow, and blue. When you mix red and yellow, you get orange. Yellow and blue make green, and blue and red make purple. Orange, green and purple are called *secondary colors*.

Mix the primary colors to make orange, green, and purple.

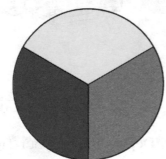 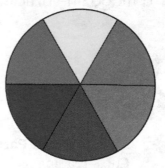

Akela's OK   Date   Recorded by the den leader

Note to Adult Partner: Boys can use nontoxic paints, clay, food coloring, or crayons for this activity. For some extra fun, have boys think of animals of different colors and put them on a color wheel. They might think of red squirrels, green lizards, blue birds, yellow birds, or orange fish.

Collecting and Other Hobbies

It is fun to learn about the collections and hobbies of your friends. They like to hear about your interests, too. Tell your den about something you like to collect or do for fun.

With your den, show or tell about something you like to collect
 OR
 Tell your den about a favorite hobby or activity.

| Akela's OK | | Date | Recorded by the den leader |

Note to Adult Partner: This is an excellent den activity. But even if your den doesn't plan this activity, your Tiger Cub can still complete this elective by asking the den leader whether he can take a few minutes during a den meeting to share his collection or hobby with the others. Speaking to a small group helps to build a boy's confidence. While you and your Tiger Cub are preparing for this, ask him why he likes his collection or hobby. If he isn't sure, you can share your hobbies with him and tell him what you like best about them. Do you and your Tiger Cub share a common interest or hobby?

ELECTIVE 17

Make a Model

Many models are made out of wood or plastic. But you can make a model out of almost anything: clay, papier-mâché, or recycled materials. You can make a model of a car, boat, house, bird, or apple. There is no limit to the number of things you can make! If you participate in a pinewood derby, space derby, or raingutter regatta with your pack, you can count it for this elective.

Make a model.

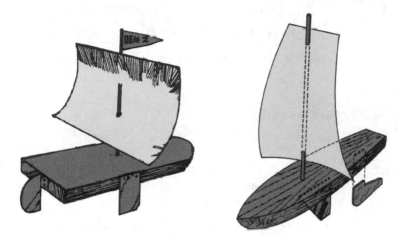

17 Akela's OK   Date   Recorded by the den leader

Note to Adult Partner: This activity is excellent as either a den or a family activity. Your boy can assemble an easy purchased model kit, or he can mold a model with clay. Making models improves his spatial and fine motor skills and allows him to be creative, too. Why not make your own model with him while he does his?

18 Sew a Button

It is handy to know how to sew on a button. The more you practice, the neater your sewing will be.

Sew a button onto fabric.

Materials: An assortment of buttons with two or four holes, fabric scraps, needle with a large eye, sewing thread

Cut a piece of thread about 20 inches long and thread the end into the needle. Double the thread and make a knot in the end. Put the button on the cloth where you want it, and hold it there with one hand. With the other, bring the needle up through one of the holes of the button from the wrong side and pull gently until the thread is all the way through the cloth. Then push the needle through another hole back to the wrong side of the fabric. Keep working the thread up and down through the holes until the button is secure. End with the needle on the wrong side and make a knot by taking several small stitches in the same spot. Cut off the extra thread.

Note to Adult Partner: Depending on your Tiger Cub's manual dexterity, you may have to guide him quite a bit at first. Encourage him to keep practicing, and praise him often as he improves. If you think he would enjoy it, suggest that he make a simple design on the fabric with buttons, such as a triangle or a zigzag pattern.

ELECTIVE 19

Magic Fun

Magic tricks just look like they cannot be explained because they "trick" our eyes. The more you practice a trick, the better you will be able to make your audience think it is true magic.

Learn a magic trick and show it to your family or den.

Magic Jumping Paper Clips

Materials: Dollar bill, two paper clips

Fold the bill into three parts and clip each fold with the corner nearest to it, as shown. Take the top corners, A and B, between your thumbs and fingers. Pull the bill out straight. The clips will join with each other and jump off!

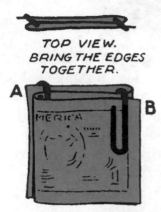

TOP VIEW.
BRING THE EDGES
TOGETHER.

MAKE THE FOLDS
SHARP.

Magic Unbreakable Balloon

Materials: Balloons, clear cellophane tape, straight pins

Blow up a balloon and stick a piece of tape on it. Hide the taped area and tell your audience that you are going to put a pin in the balloon but that it will not break. Gently push the pin through the tape into the balloon and amaze your audience.

19   _____   _____
      Akela's OK   Date   Recorded by the den leader

Note to Adult Partner: This activity helps your Tiger Cub build confidence and become more comfortable in front of an audience. Be ready to help him if he falters, making sure that he has a successful experience. You can find more magic tricks in *Cub Scout Magic* and the *Cub Scout Leader How-To Book*.

Get the Word Out

We see a lot of advertisements on TV and other media. Advertisements tell people about something and usually are trying to persuade them to buy a product. But some advertisements, called *public service announcements,* or PSAs, give people information that can help their lives or help them be better citizens. A PSA might tell you about the dangers of smoking, or it might tell you where to get help in your community if you need it.

With your den, make up a PSA skit to tell people about Tiger Cubs.

In your skit, tell the audience why you like Tiger Cubs and why they should join, too.

Tell them how it will help their lives. Remember that Tiger Cubs are always kind and never make fun of other people—even in skits. Your den leader may ask the Cubmaster whether you can perform your Tiger Cub PSA at the next pack meeting.

20 | Akela's OK _____ | Date ____ | Recorded by the den leader ____

Note to Adult Partner: Performing in front of an audience helps your Tiger Cub build self-confidence. Help him practice his part in the skit, and be prepared to prompt him if he needs it. Discuss advertisements and PSAs with your Tiger Cub. What are some of the differences?

ELECTIVE

21 The Show Must Go On

It is fun to pretend that you are a different person or an animal. One way to do this is to make a puppet and pretend that the puppet can talk. After you make your puppet, you might want to put on a puppet show for your family or with your den.

Make a puppet.

You can make a paper bag puppet or a paper plate puppet, or you can use a different idea of your own.

Talking Paper Bag Puppet

Materials: Paper lunch bags, crayons, felt-tip markers, construction paper, yarn, buttons, scissors, glue

Leave the bag folded. Place it fold-side up on a table. Mark where you want eyes and nose and other features to go. The eyes, nose, and the top of the mouth should go on the bottom of the bag, and the bottom of the mouth should go on the front of the bag, as shown. Glue on hair, ears, clothing—decorate your puppet as you want. When you put your hand on the inside, you can make your puppet talk.

Paper Plate Puppet

Materials: Paper plate, paint stirring stick, heavy tape, markers, glue, craft items (glitter, yarn buttons, etc.)

Draw whatever kind of face you want on a paper plate. Glue or tape yarn for hair, glitter for freckles, etc. Then tape the paint stick to the back of the paper plate.

21 Akela's OK _____ Date _____ Recorded by the den leader

Note to Adult Partner: This activity can provide hours of fun for boys. They can perform skits with their puppets, or they might want to make a puppet of the animal they learned about in Elective 31, "Learn About Animals." Encourage your Tiger Cub to show his puppet to others.

Picnic Fun

Have you ever had a picnic? Was it outdoors? Most picnics are outdoors, but you can have a picnic indoors, too.

With your family or with your den, have a picnic—outdoors or indoors.

Akela's OK _____ Date _____ Recorded by the den leader

Note to Adult Partner: A traditional outdoor picnic can be a lot of fun for your den or family. This gives you the opportunity to play outdoor games and appreciate nature with your Tiger Cub. For an indoor picnic, spread a blanket on the floor, draw ants on small pieces of paper, and eat traditional picnic foods. Encourage your Tiger Cub to use his imagination and to pretend that he is getting hot in the sun or that it is windy and blowing away paper plates and cups. He can protect his food from the "ants" and pretend that lamps are trees. You could even pretend that it starts raining suddenly and see how fast you can clean up to get out of the "rain." Play along and have fun with him.

ELECTIVE 23
What Kind of Milk?

When you go to the store to buy milk, you will see many choices. Most of the milk we drink comes from cows. You can buy skim, 1 percent, 2 percent, or whole (4 percent) milk. The percentage tells you how much fat is in the milk. You can buy buttermilk, soy milk, or lactose-free milk. You can even buy powdered milk. Some milk is flavored, such as chocolate or strawberry milk. Milk comes in all sizes of containers, and the containers can be made of glass, plastic, or waxy cardboard.

Find out what kind of milk your family drinks and why.

Akela's OK _____ Date ____ Recorded by the den leader

Note to Adult Partner: Discuss all aspects of your family milk choice, including taste, nutrition, possible allergic reactions, containers (size, type, cost), and convenience. If possible, let your Tiger Cub taste different kinds of milk. This could be a good den activity.

Help in the Kitchen

Many things need to be done to prepare a meal for your family—from setting the table before the meal, preparing the food to eat, and then cleaning up after the meal.

Help the adult who is preparing a family meal to set the table and to clean up afterward.

Akela's OK _____ Date _____ Recorded by the den leader

Note to Adult Partner: This activity reinforces the fact that family members should do their part to help each other. It also gives a boy a better understanding of all the things that adults do to prepare and serve a meal. This can be a time for you and your Tiger Cub to talk about what you did during the day. Remember to thank the Tiger Cub for his help.

Snack Time

We all like to eat snacks. But it is also fun to make snacks and to share them with others.

Make a snack and share it with your family or den.

Ocean Bottom Crackers

Ingredients: Round snack crackers, fish-shaped crackers, cream cheese (or Neufchâtel cheese), blue food coloring

Mix a drop or two of blue food coloring in softened cream cheese. Spread it on round crackers for your "ocean." Then put a fish cracker on top of the cream cheese.

Patriotic Surprise

Ingredients: Blueberries, sliced strawberries (or any other red berry), cottage cheese (or any other white food, such as coconut flakes)

Wash your hands with soap and warm water. Then arrange the red, white, and blue foods to form a U.S. flag.

Ants on a Log

Ingredients: Celery; peanut butter or soft cheese or cream cheese spread; raisins *or* dried cranberries

Cut the celery into sticks. Fill the middles with peanut butter or cheese. Put fruit "ants" on the peanut butter or cheese and enjoy!

25

Akela's OK	Date	Recorded by the den leader

Note to Adult Partner: The above snacks are suggestions. Boys may make any snack, but make sure that it is nutritious and that it is not too hard for boys to prepare. Always check before serving food to be sure that no one in the group has allergies, such as to peanuts or certain fruits. (Some allergies can be life-threatening!) Boys love to help in the kitchen, and they are proud when others enjoy eating what they have made. Look for opportunities to have your Tiger Cub help with meal or snack preparation. He will learn and have fun, and you will have more time with him.

Phone Manners

Telephones are not toys. You need to learn good phone manners.

With a toy phone, or a disconnected phone, practice making phone calls and answering the telephone.

Always follow the rules set by the adults in your family about how to use and answer the phone.

> Emergency : 911
> Police : 345-5555
> Fire Department : 683-5555
> Mom at work : 345-4554
> Dr. Casey : 688-6729
> Mr. & Mrs. Douglas next door : 345-2233

26   Akela's OK _____   Date _____ Recorded by the den leader

Note to Adult Partner: It's good for your Tiger Cub to become comfortable with how to use a telephone. Allow him to practice his skills often, but be clear about family rules for phone usage by children. You may help him make a simple list of emergency and family phone numbers, and then have him place it near the phone.

Emergency!

We never expect bad things to happen, but sometimes they do. It is good to be prepared for emergencies and dangerous situations.

Talk with your adult partner about what to do if these things happened:

- The adult who is caring for you becomes ill.
- You are alone with someone who makes you feel uncomfortable.

Akela's OK   Date   Recorded by the den leader

Note to Adult Partner: Talk with your Tiger Cub about the above situations. Make it a habit to talk with him regularly about these and other potentially harmful situations, such as what should you do if a neighbor boy wants to show you his dad's gun while you and he are alone in the house? Why shouldn't you tease a dog?

Smoke Detectors

Smoke detectors can help save your life by warning you of a fire before it gets too big. But the smoke detector cannot do its job if it is not working.

With your adult partner, check the batteries in the smoke detector in your home or another building.

28 _____ | Akela's OK | Date | Recorded by the den leader

Note to Adult Partner: Smoke detectors should be checked annually. A good way to remember is to check it at the same time each year. For instance, each fall you could check your smoke detector when you set your clocks back. Or check it at some other special time, such as on your birthday or on a holiday. If your Tiger Cub helps you with this, he will develop this habit, too.

29 Safety in the Sun

Your skin is an important part of your body. It protects you from infection and when it is exposed to sunlight, it produces vitamin D, which is important for good health. Moderately exposing your skin to the sun in good weather is important, and playing outdoors when the weather is warm and sunny is fun. But too much sun can hurt your skin. When you are near water, it is especially important to protect your skin because the rays of the sun reflect off the water and can hurt your skin even more. Hot summer days are not the only times when you can get a sunburn. You can get a sunburn on cloudy days—and even when playing in the snow! It is important to wear sunscreen to protect yourself from the harmful rays of the sun.

Use an SPF 15 or stronger sunscreen that shields against both UVA and UVB rays. Apply the sunscreen 15 to 20 minutes before going outside and reapply every two hours.

Talk with your adult partner about when you should use sunscreen. Find out whether you have any in your home and where it is kept. With your adult partner, look at a container of sunscreen and find out whether it still protects you when you are wet. Also find out how long you are protected before you have to put on more. Look for the expiration date and make sure the sunscreen is not too old.

Note to Adult Partner: Protection from overexposure to the sun is very important. Children learn by watching what we do. Set a good example by using sunscreen yourself when you are out in the sun.

30   Plant a Seed

It is fun to watch plants grow. Have you ever planted a pit or seed from something you have eaten?

Plant a seed, pit, or green tops from something you have eaten.

Here are a few things you might try:

Avocado pit: Insert three toothpicks into the pit as shown. Make sure the small end of the pit is pointing up and place it in a glass of water. You can plant it in soil when it has grown long roots.

Carrot: Choose carrots at the grocery store that still have greens on the tops. Cut the greens to about ½ inch. Remove any old green leaves from the tops. Cut the orange part of the carrot to about 1 inch, and eat the rest. Place the carrot top in a flat dish that is filled with either fish gravel or sand and water. You may want to place several carrot tops in the dish. Put the dish in a sunny place, and soon tender new shoots will appear.

Orange or other citrus seed: After eating an orange (or tangerine or grapefruit or other citrus fruit), soak the seeds in water for a day to clean and moisten them. Place a few stones in the bottom of a garden pot or any container with small holes in the bottom. Fill with potting soil and poke holes into the soil about ½ inch deep with your finger. Put one seed in each hole and cover them with soil. Put the pot onto a saucer or drip container to catch any water that may drip out when you water it. Put it in a sunny place and remember to keep the soil moist by watering it.

You might also try to grow apple seeds, pear seeds, potatoes, sweet potatoes, pineapple tops, pumpkin seeds, and beet tops.

30

Note to Adult Partner: Watering plants regularly teaches your Tiger Cub responsibility. If you have an area where you can plant seeds outside, your boy can try transplanting some of his plants outdoors after they start growing.

Learn About Animals

31

You may know a lot about some animals. But there are a lot of animals to learn about. Choose an animal that you would like to learn more about for this activity.

Learn about an animal.

With your adult partner, use books, magazines, or the Internet to learn the following things about your animal:

- How big is it?
- Where does it live?
- What kind of food does it eat?

- How long does it usually live?
- What sounds does it make?
- Is it endangered?

31   Akela's OK   Date   Recorded by the den leader

Note to Adult Partner: By doing this activity, Tiger Cubs will not only learn about an animal but also will be able to practice research skills. He could make a puppet for Elective 21, "The Show Must Go On," to resemble this animal.

ELECTIVE

32   Feed the Birds

Birds and other outdoor animals need to eat food every day just like you do. If you put up a bird feeder, you can watch the birds enjoy a meal.

Make a bird feeder and then hang it outdoors.

You can make any kind of bird feeder. Here are two suggestions that birds would like.

Pinecone Bird Feeder

Materials: ½ cup peanut butter, ½ cup shortening, 1 to 2 cups bird seed, large pinecone, thick twine, paper bag

Twist the twine around the pinecone and tie it securely. Mix the peanut butter and shortening together. Spread the mixture between the scales of the pinecone, filling in as much as you can. Put the pinecone along with the bird seed in the paper bag. Close the bag and shake it, coating the pinecone with bird seed. Hang the feeder on a tree where you can watch the birds enjoy it.

If you do not have pinecones, you can do the same thing with a cardboard toilet tissue tube. Punch two holes in one end (opposite each other), and thread a string through for hanging. Spread with the peanut butter/shortening mixture, and roll the tube in seeds.

Garland for the Birds

Materials: Oranges, day-old bread, heavy-duty twine, yarn needle

Tear the bread slices into quarters. Slice the oranges into rounds, and then cut each round in quarters. Thread

the needle with about a yard of thread and string the food in a pattern, leaving a few inches between foods. Head outside to decorate a bush or tree with natural goodies for winter birds.

32   Akela's OK   Date   Recorded by the den leader

Note to Adult Partner: This simple activity could lead to a lifelong hobby of bird watching. Encourage your Tiger Cub to keep his new feeder full and share the following safety tips with him while you are helping him assemble his feeder:

- Cover anything sharp on the feeder.
- Never use thread, as birds can easily become entangled.
- Always use fresh, clean grains and seeds, as moldy food can make birds sick.
- Do not paint your feeder.
- Do not use plain peanut butter, as it is harmful to the digestive system of the birds. Always mix peanut butter with another fat or oil.

ELECTIVE

33 Cleanup Treasure Hunt

Work can be more fun when you turn it into a game. Even helping to clean up can be a game. When you play Cleanup Treasure Hunt, not only will you have fun looking for things, but you will also help the environment.

Electives

> With your den or family, play Cleanup Treasure Hunt.

Cleanup Treasure Hunt

Materials: Gloves, trash bags, photocopies of a "treasure" list of different kinds of litter, pencils

You should have two teams of two or more people. Each team should have gloves, two trash bags, and a copy of a "treasure" list. Set a time limit. Carefully pick up all the litter you find and place it in a trash bag. As you find items on your list, check them off. When the time is up, the team with the most items from the treasure list wins. Pick out the items that can be recycled, and properly dispose of the rest of the litter. Some items to include on your treasure lists could be a candy wrapper, empty pop cans, paper, bottle tops, foil items, or plastic foam items.

Akela's OK _____   Date   Recorded by the den leader

Note to Adult Partner: It's never too early to teach your Tiger Cub the importance of doing his part to keep his community clean. While you are teaching him to be a good citizen, remind him to be safe and always handle litter with gloves on. After you play Cleanup Treasure Hunt, ask your Tiger Cub how he felt about helping to clean up. Ask him why he thinks people litter.

34 Conservation

Our planet has a number of natural resources, such as water, gas, and oil. It is important for us to be careful how we use these resources because they could run out. This is called *conservation*.

With your adult partner, think of a way to conserve water or electricity and do it for one week.

Here are two suggestions:

- Collect rainwater and use it to water plants in your home.
- Turn out the lights and turn off the TV or radio when you are not in a room.

34 | Akela's OK _____ | Date | Recorded by the den leader _____

Note to Adult Partner: Conservation of natural resources is a very big concept for a first-grade boy. The object of this activity is to make him aware of what he uses and encourage him to not waste resources. If you feel that he is mature enough to understand, you might share with him your views about the earth and its resources.

Fun Outdoors

It is fun to play outdoors! Most games that you can play indoors, you can play outdoors, too. You can play games with balls or games that make you run, jump, hop, and skip. You can play with one other person, or you can play with lots of people. The possibilities are endless!

Play a game outdoors with your family or den.

Akela's OK _____ Date   Recorded by the den leader

Note to Adult Partner: Cub Scouting offers many exciting summertime activities, such as Cub Scout day camp, Cub Scout resident camp, and various pack activities. Find out from your den leader what types of activities your pack has planned for the summer.

See a Performance

36

Seeing a live performance is exciting!

With your family or your den, go see a play or musical performance in your community.

36

| Akela's OK | Date | Recorded by the den leader |

ELECTIVE 37

Take a Bicycle Ride

Riding a bicycle is good exercise, and it is fun!

Take a bicycle ride with your adult partner.

You can do this along with other family members or with your den. Make sure that you wear a helmet!

37 | Akela's OK | | Date | Recorded by the den leader

Note to Adult Partner: Regular exercise is important for keeping a body healthy. Bicycle riding is good exercise and provides plenty of fresh air. As an added benefit, our natural resources are conserved and pollution is lessened when people walk or ride a bicycle as an alternative to riding a car or bus for transportation. But to your Tiger Cub, riding a bicycle is just plain fun! *Remember:* Boys must *always* wear a helmet when they ride a bike!

Bicycle Repair

Bicycles must be kept in good working condition so that they are safe and can be used a long time. Broken bicycles can often be fixed. People at a bicycle repair shop know how bicycles work and know how to fix and take care of them. You can talk with them and learn about bicycles.

Visit a bicycle repair shop.

See how people fix broken bicycles and what they do to keep them working. Find out what you can do to take care of a bicycle so that it will last a long time.

38

Akela's OK	Date Recorded by the den leader

Note to Adult Partner: Many bicycle stores have maintenance and repair centers. When visiting, ask a mechanic to tell the Tiger Cubs what they can do to keep their bicycles in good working condition.

Go to Work

Do you ever wonder what adults do at work?

Visit the place where your adult partner or another adult works.

39

Akela's OK   Date   Recorded by the den leader

Note to Adult Partner: If the den visits the workplace of one of the adult partners in the den, each boy can count this elective as completed.

Fun in the Water

Swimming is good exercise, and it is fun, too. Learning how to swim is also very important for your personal safety.

Together with your adult partner, go swimming or take part in an activity in water.

40 Akela's OK _____   Date   Recorded by the den leader

Note to Adult Partner: Set a good example for your Tiger Cub by following safe swimming rules. (Check with your den leader or Cubmaster for information about BSA's Safe Swim Defense policies.) Never swim in water without a lifeguard or other adult present.

Don't swim just after a large meal or if you are very tired. Be sure to protect yourself from the sun (see Elective 29). If your Tiger Cub doesn't know how to swim, think about a plan to teach him or take him to swimming lessons. It will give him confidence in the water and could save his life someday. Check with your den leader to see whether your activity may qualify your Tiger Cub for recognition as part of the Cub Scout Academics and Sports program.

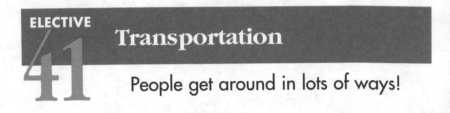

Transportation

People get around in lots of ways!

Visit a train station, bus station, airport, or boat dock.

41 Akela's OK

Date   Recorded by the den leader

Note to Adult Partner: When you are alone with your Tiger Cub, you can travel with him on any form of transportation you choose. But when you are with your den, you must follow the Boy Scouts of America rules for that activity. Check with your den leader or Cubmaster for the publication *Guide to Safe Scouting*, which include rules and guidelines for safe Scouting functions. (Or read it on-line: www.scouting.org/pubs/gss)

ELECTIVE

42 Fun at the Zoo

A trip to a zoo or an aquarium is fun, and you will always learn something new.

Visit a zoo or aquarium.

42 Akela's OK _____ Date _____ Recorded by the den leader

Note to Adult Partner: Boys love to visit zoos and aquariums. Before going, find out whether it has educational programs for children.

43 Pet Care

Having a pet is fun, but it is also a lot of work to take care of a pet.

Visit a veterinarian or an animal groomer.

Note to Adult Partner: Having a pet is a big responsibility. If your Tiger Cub has a pet, encourage him to be involved in caring for it. When you visit the veterinarian or groomer, ask him or her what is involved in caring for different kinds of pets.

ELECTIVE

Dairy Products

44

You probably know that the milk we drink usually comes from cows, but have you seen how the milk is processed and put into bottles or cartons for us?

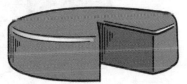

Visit a dairy, a milk-processing plant, or a cheese factory.

44 <u>Akela's OK</u>   <u>Date</u>   <u>Recorded by the den leader</u>

 Note to Adult Partner: Elective 23, "What Kind of Milk?," fits nicely with this activity.

ELECTIVE

45 Fresh Baking

Although you may buy bread and cakes at the grocery store, they are baked at a bakery.

Visit a bakery.

Note to Adult Partner: For this activity, you may visit any place where foods are baked. You may visit a small local bakery or a large baking company. Some large grocery stores bake their own goods. After your visit, you may want to bake cookies at home or read the ingredients of baked goods that you buy.

Healthy Teeth and Gums

You need to take care of your teeth and gums now so that they will stay healthy your whole life. Without healthy teeth and gums, you will not have a nice, big smile.

Visit a dentist or dental hygienist.

Ask what you can do to take care of your teeth and gums. Ask the person what he or she had to learn about the job that they do.

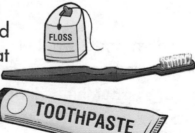

Note to Adult Partner: A get-acquainted visit to the dentist without dental work to be done can help your boy feel more relaxed when he goes to the dentist to have his teeth looked at. He can learn about the office and can also learn that the dentist or hygienist is nice and wants to help him. Note that such a visit may require an appointment.

ELECTIVE

47 Reduce, Reuse, Recycle

When we recycle, we help our environment. Lots of items can be recycled, such as newspapers, aluminum and tin cans, cardboard, glass, and plastics. You can even recycle old clothes that do not fit you anymore so that someone else can wear them.

Learn about what you can recycle in your community and how you can recycle at home. Learn about things that need to be recycled in special ways, such as paint and batteries.

In some communities, items to be recycled can be placed in special boxes at the curb along with trash. In other communities, you take your recyclable items to a central location.

47 | Akela's OK _____ | Date | Recorded by the den leader _____

Note to Adult Partner: Encouraging boys to learn and think about recycling will help them start a lifelong habit of conservation that will help protect our environment.

Go for a Ride

48

Public transportation is a good way to get around. Most public transportation systems have buses, but some have trains and boats, too.

Take a ride on public transportation, such as a bus or train.

48

Akela's OK	Date	Recorded by the den leader

Note to Adult Partner: While you are riding, talk to your Tiger Cub about the bus or train you are on. Count or estimate how many people can travel on it at one time. Then, you might want to talk about how all those people are helping conserve natural resources and not pollute our environment by not using their cars.

Your Government

In the United States of America, we have many different levels of government. We have the federal government and state governments, as well as city and local governments.

Visit a government office such as the mayor's office, the state capitol building, or a courthouse.

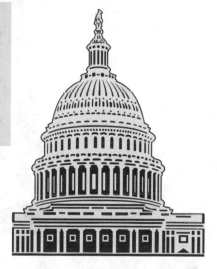

49   Akela's OK   Date   Recorded by the den leader

Note to Adult Partner: The point of this trip is to show your Tiger Cub that public servants are in place to take care of the community and make sure that laws are obeyed. You could also ask your Tiger Cub to point out the flags in the building he visits and note how they are displayed.

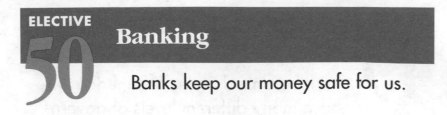

Banks keep our money safe for us.

Visit a bank.

BANK VAULT

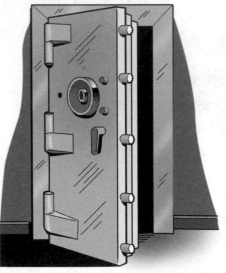

Akela's OK _____ Date _____ Recorded by the den leader

Note to Adult Partner: Ask a banker to tell your Tiger Cub what the bank does with the money that people put in their accounts. Ask how the bank uses computers. Ask how much money a Tiger Cub might have when he is 21 years old if he puts $20 in the bank when he is in first grade.

Cub Scout Outdoor Activity Award

Have you ever gotten an award for doing fun activities? That's what this award is all about! You can earn the Cub Scout Outdoor Activity Award by doing the following things.

- Attend Cub Scout day camp or Cub Scout/Webelos Scout resident camp.

- Complete one requirement in Achievement 5, "Let's Go Outdoors," and, with your den, pack, or family, complete three of the outddor activities listed below.

1. Participate in a nature hike in your local area. This can be on an organized, marked trail, or just a hike to observe nature in your area.

2. Participate in an outdoor activity such as a picnic or park fun day.

3. Explain the buddy system and tell what to do if lost. Explain the importance of cooperation.

4. Attend a pack overnighter. Be responsible by being prepared for the event.

5. Complete an outdoor service project in your community.

6. Complete a nature/conservation project in your area. This project should involve improving, beautifying, or supporting natural habitats. Discuss how this project helped you to respect nature.

7. Earn the National Summertime Pack Award pin.

8. Participate in a nature observation activity. Describe or illustrate and display your observations at a den or pack meeting.

9. Participate in an outdoor aquatic activity. Describe or illustrate and display your observations at a den or pack meeting.

10. Participate in an outdoor campfire program. Perform in a skit, sing a song, or take part in a ceremony.

11. Participate in an outdoor sporting event.

12. Participate in an outdoor interfaith worship service or other worship service.

13. Explore a local city, county, state, or national park. Discuss with your den how a good citizen obeys the park rules.

After you have done these things, ask your den leader to order your award.

Akela's OK   Date   Recorded by the den leader

Cub Scouting's Leave No Trace Awareness Award

Leave No Trace is a plan that helps you to be more concerned about your environment. It also helps you protect it for future generations.

You can earn the Cub Scouting's Leave No Trace Awareness Award by doing the following things:

1. Discuss with your leader or parent/guardian the importance of the Leave No Trace frontcountry guidelines.

2. On three separate outings, practice the frontcountry guidelines of Leave No Trace.

3. Complete Achievement 5, "Let's Go Outdoors."

4. Participate in a Leave No Trace–related service project.

5. Promise to practice the Leave No Trace frontcountry guidelines by signing the Cub Scout Leave No Trace Pledge.

6. Draw a poster to illustrate the Leave No Trace frontcountry guidelines and display it at a pack meeting.

After you have done these things, ask your den leader to order your award.

Cub Scout Leave No Trace Pledge

I promise to practice the Leave No Trace front-country guidelines wherever I go:

1. Plan ahead.
2. Stick to trails.
3. Manage your pet.
4. Leave what you find.
5. Respect other visitors.
6. Trash your trash.

_____
Signed

_____   _____   _____
Akela's OK   Date   Recorded by the den leader

Note to Adult Partner: Ask your den leader for more information on Cub Scouting's Leave No Trace frontcountry guidelines and this award.

Cub Scout Academics and Sports

You can have fun and learn new skills when you take part in the Cub Scout Academics and Sports program. Just by learning about and participating in a sport or academic subject, you can earn belt loops and pins.

Each academic and sport subject is included in the *Cub Scout Academics and Sports Program Guide,* which tells you what the requirements are for earning the special recognition of belt loops and pins.

You can take part in the program at home, in your den or pack, or in activities in your community. Archery and BB-gun shooting are restricted to day camps, Cub Scout/ Webelos Scout resident camps, council-managed family camping programs, or to council activities where there are properly trained supervisors and all standards for BSA shooting sports are enforced. Ask your den leader to tell you more about the Cub Scout Academics and Sports program and the 40 Academics and Sports subjects that you can explore!

Academics

Art

Astronomy

Chess

Citizenship

Collecting

Communicating

Computers

Geography

Geology

Heritages

Language
and Culture

Map and
Compass

Mathematics

Music

Science

Weather

Wildlife
Conservation

Sports

Badminton

Baseball

Basketball

Bicycling

Bowling

Fishing

Flag Football

Golf

Gymnastics

Ice Skating

Marbles

Physical
Fitness

Roller
Skating

Snow Ski and
Board Sports

Soccer

Softball

Swimming

Table Tennis

Tennis

Ultimate

Volleyball

Your adult partner can find out more information in the *Cub Scout Academics and Sports Program Guide* (No. 34299) about how you can work on earning belt loops and pins.

As a Tiger Cub, I have earned these Cub Scout Academics and Sports belt loops:

_____

_____

_____

_____

_____

_____

_____

_____

_____

Cub Scouting's BSA Family Program

The BSA Family program is a series of activities designed to help strengthen all families—whether two-parent, single-parent, or nontraditional families. All family members are encouraged to participate and earn the BSA Family Award.

A Cub Scouting family may choose to participate in this program on its own, or the pack may choose to introduce the program to families through a pack orientation.

Cub Scouting's BSA Family Activity Book (No. 33012A) is the primary resource for the program. The book is divided into five categories that include many topics of interest to families. Additional family activity ideas are presented monthly in *Scouting* magazine, which is sent to all registered leaders. These discussion ideas help to strengthen family communication and values.

To earn the BSA Family Award, a family completes 10 activities in 12 months. The family chooses one activity in two topics in each of five categories:

Family Activity Topics

1. Learning Through Fun and Adventure
Enjoying Family Fun
Knowing It's Make-Believe
Cultivating Talents
Being Patriotic

2. Strengthening Family Relationships
Making Mealtime Meaningful
Strengthening Family Traditions
Understanding Siblings
Showing Love
Communicating
Sharing

3. Developing Character
Learning Duty to God
Fostering Self-Esteem
Accepting Success
Trusting
Giving
Accepting Differences

4. Teaching Responsibility
Developing Responsibility
Being Prepared
Planning and Organizing
Managing Money

5. Handling Difficult Situations
Overcoming Obstacles
Adjusting to a Move
Coping With Long-Term Illness
Loss of Loved Ones

The BSA Family Award includes a certificate for the family as well as patches and pins for family members. The recognitions should be presented to the family at the pack meeting.

Transition to a Wolf Den

Transition to a Wolf Den

At the end of the Tiger Cub year, the Tiger Cub den will take part in a ceremony at a pack meeting. This ceremony marks the transition to the next level of Cub Scouting: a Wolf den. Your Tiger Cub den leader will plan for this ceremony along with the Cubmaster.

Once a Tiger Cub has been recognized in this ceremony for completion of his Tiger Cub year, he can no longer work on Tiger Cub requirements. He now works on the Wolf advancement requirements outlined in the *Wolf Handbook.* This is the next step in Cub Scouting. The Wolf program is designed for second-grade (or 8-year old) boys and is more challenging than the Tiger Cub program. While in a Wolf den, he will take part in fun and educational activities related to the monthly theme, and advancement will be done at home with his family. Each year, as a boy progresses through the Cub Scout ranks, the program will grow with him to meet his needs as he develops.

This is also a good time for the Tiger Cub adult partner to consider taking a position on the pack leadership team. There are many opportunities for helping with Cub Scouting, and your boy will be more successful and enjoy his Cub Scouting experience more if members of his family are there along with him. But when your boy moves up to a Wolf den, your registration as a Tiger Cub partner ends, and you will need to complete an adult registration form to remain registered with your pack.

It's Time to Start on the Wolf Cub Scout Trail!

(For the boy, to be read by his adult partner)

Wow! You're finishing first grade and you've finished your Tiger Cub year! You're growing up fast! It's time to move on to the next step in Cub Scouting. You and the other boys in your den will now start on the trail to becoming a Wolf Cub Scout. You can put this handbook away and start working on the activities in the *Wolf Handbook.*

Congratulations! You did a great job this year!

Trails to Advancement

Tiger Cub Immediate Recognition

Color each tiger paw print as you move along the Tiger Trail.

 I know the Cub Scout motto.

Akela's OK	Date	Recorded by the den leader

 I know the Cub Scout sign.

Akela's OK	Date	Recorded by the den leader

 I know the Cub Scout salute.

Akela's OK	Date	Recorded by the den leader

When you have colored all three of the tiger tracks, you will have earned your Tiger Cub Immediate Recognition Emblem.

Bobcat Trail

1. The Cub Scout Promise and the Honesty Character Connection

2. The Law of the Pack

3. The meaning of Weblos

4. The Cub Scout sign

5. The Cub Scout handshake

6. The Cub Scout motto

7. The Cub Scout salute

8. "A Bobcat Requirement"

When you have colored all eight of the bobcat paw prints, you will have earned your Bobcat badge.

Tiger Cub Badge Trail

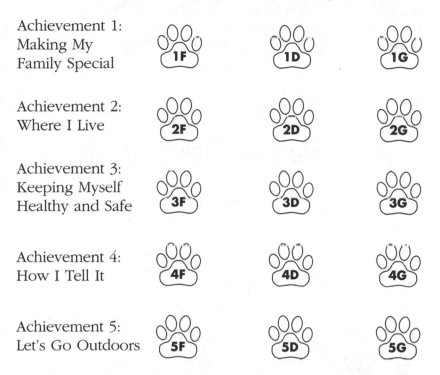

	Family Activity	Den Activity	Go See It
Achievement 1: Making My Family Special	1F	1D	1G
Achievement 2: Where I Live	2F	2D	2G
Achievement 3: Keeping Myself Healthy and Safe	3F	3D	3G
Achievement 4: How I Tell It	4F	4D	4G
Achievement 5: Let's Go Outdoors	5F	5D	5G

When you have colored all 15 of the tiger paw prints, you will have earned your Tiger Cub badge.

Tiger Track Trail

Each time you complete an elective, write that number in a tiger track. Each time you complete 10 electives, color the tiger track at the end of the row that says "I did it!" Tell your den leader, and you will receive a Tiger track bead.

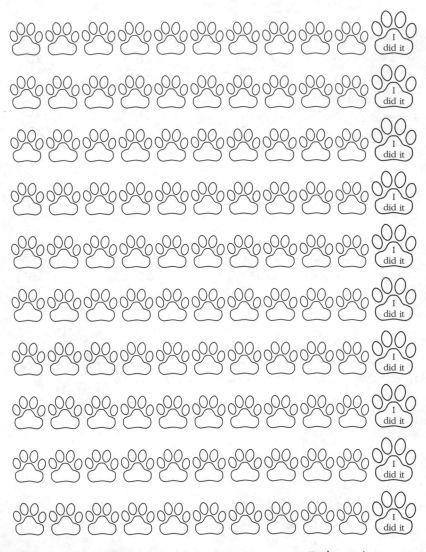